Donated by an Anonymous
friend

W9-BYF-639

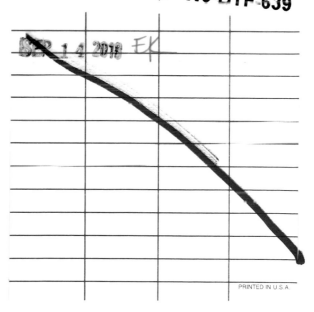

SEP 1 4 2010 EK

PRINTED IN U.S.A.

Morningstar

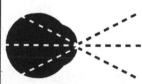

This Large Print Book carries the
Seal of Approval of N.A.V.H.

MORNINGSTAR

GROWING UP WITH BOOKS

ANN HOOD

THORNDIKE PRESS
A part of Gale, Cengage Learning

GALE
CENGAGE Learning·

Farmington Hills, Mich • San Francisco • New York • Waterville, Maine
Meriden, Conn • Mason, Ohio • Chicago

GALE
CENGAGE Learning·

LIBRARY OF CONGRESS CATALOGING-IN-PUBLICATION DATA

Names: Hood, Ann, 1956– author.
Title: Morningstar : growing up with books / by Ann Hood.
Description: Large print edition. | Waterville, Maine : Thorndike Press, a part
  of Gale, a Cengage Company, 2017. | Series: Thorndike Press large print
  biographies and memoirs
Identifiers: LCCN 2017030291| ISBN 9781432844066 (hardcover) | ISBN
  1432844067 (hardcover)
Subjects: LCSH: Hood, Ann, 1956– —Books and reading. | Novelists,
  American—20th century—Biography. | Books and reading. | Large type
  books.
Classification: LCC PS3558.O537 Z46 2017b | DDC 813/.54 [B] —dc23
LC record available at https://lccn.loc.gov/2017030291

Published in 2017 by arrangement with W. W. Norton & Company, Inc.

Printed in Mexico
1 2 3 4 5 6 7 21 20 19 18 17

*This book is for all the giants
whose shoulders I stand on —
With thanks for letting me
see farther*

CONTENTS

INTRODUCTION:
*Growing Up
with Books.* 9

Lesson 1: How to Dream . . . 43
Lesson 2: How to Become a
    Writer 64
Lesson 3: How to Ask Why . . 96
Lesson 4: How to Buy
    Books 123
Lesson 5: How to Write
    a Book 140

Lesson 6: How to Fall in
    Love with Language . . . 167
Lesson 7: How to Be
    Curious. 190
Lesson 8: How to Have
    Sex. 219
Lesson 9: How to See the
    World. 249
Lesson 10: How to Run
    Away 275

ACKNOWLEDGMENTS. . . 297

INTRODUCTION:
GROWING UP WITH BOOKS

When I was four years old, for reasons no one in my family could explain, I picked up my older brother Skip's reading book and I read it. This was in 1959 or 1960, but I can still remember staring at that page and reading the words *Look! Look!* In that instant, all of my cells seemed to settle into place and I had one thought: *I want to live inside a book.*

I did not grow up in a family that owned books. My great-grandparents had immigrated from Italy in the late 1800s as part of the large exodus of southern Italian farm laborers who, burdened by heavy taxes, low pay, and harsh living conditions, came to the United States to work in the mills for higher wages and security. Their daughter, my grandmother Mama Rose, left school in third grade for a job in the big textile mill that loomed over the neighborhood. She never learned to read or write, except for her slow, careful, seemingly painful signature. Of her ten children, their education interrupted by the death of their father and the start of World War II, only three graduated from high school. The girls all went to work in various factories — making artificial flowers or luggage or soap; the boys became barbers or mechanics. Reading was not something for which they had time or inclination.

My father, a small-town Indiana boy from a family of nine, dropped out of high school to join the navy and see the world. He had a love for cheap paperbacks that he read at sea, Zane Grey and James Cain. But I never saw him read a book at home. In fact, I never saw *anyone* read a book at home.

Yet I did grow up with stories, stories told around the kitchen table on Saturday afternoons or after dinner during the week. Aunts and uncles, great-aunts and -uncles, cousins and second cousins and cousins twice removed, relatives with confusing family ties, all sat and drank black coffee and talked into the night. I learned early that you had to earn your place at that table. Your story had to start with a hook, include vivid details, have strong characters, and be full of tension or someone who talked louder and could tell her story better would overpower you. Truman Capote said that he learned how to write a story not from reading but from sitting on his aunts' front porch in Alabama and listening to them tell stories. This was my earliest education in the art of storytelling too.

But I yearned for another kind of story, the kind I found in books.

When I was very young, each village in our town had its own library. These villages had all evolved around mills, and they had their own ethnic population: the French-Canadians and Irish and Italian and Portuguese and Polish, each a chapter in our town's own immigrant history. The Italians lived in Natick, and the Natick Library sat in a basement on a sad dead-end street on the banks of the Pawtuxet River, the river that led to all the mills being built in West Warwick and all the immigrants — like my great-grandparents — who flocked there for work. When I was a young child, the Pawtuxet River was brown and sluggish, topped by a yellowish foam. It flooded frequently. The books in that small library smelled of polluted water and mold and dank cellar air. I only got to go there a few times in first grade before it was shut down for good, but I remember picking up the books and bringing them to my nose, inhaling deeply. To me, that terrible smell was wonderful.

My small school at the bottom of the hill where our house was perched had no school library. Instead, each teacher had books on shelves in the back of the classroom — books we were not allowed to read until we'd finished all of our class work: the smudged blue mimeographed worksheets, the arithmetic written in pencil on small rectangular off-white paper, the connect-the-dots alphabet on yellow lined paper. I found it hard to concentrate on any of it. The books behind me seemed to whisper for me to come. I would glance over my shoulder, a fat pink eraser clutched in my hand, and read the titles, already trying to choose which one I'd read when I finally — finally! — finished my times tables.

It's hard to describe the magic that books held for me then. Even our class reading books brought me my happiest moments at school. I was an awkward, shy kid. Bad at sports and ignorant of playground etiquette, I usually sat alone on the blacktop and played jacks during recess, swiping up the shiny jacks and small red ball over and over so often that the side of my right hand was always scraped. But when Miss Dwyer or Mrs. McMahon announced it was time to get into our reading groups, I was always the first one to pick up my chair and sit in the circle, book immediately open in my lap. If my teacher had to go to the bathroom, she would order the class to take out their reading books and announce that Ann was going to read aloud until she got back. What pleasure I took in that, even though no one listened as I read. I didn't care. I was in the world of stories and words, a world I preferred to the classroom or playground.

But what is a child who loves

books that much supposed to do when she has no access to them? Every week at home *Time* magazine arrived, and every month we got *Reader's Digest.* In the early evening, just before supper, the paperboy brought the evening newspaper. And so my earliest reading was "Milestones" in *Time;* "Life in These United States," "Humor in Uniform," "Drama in Real Life," and "How to Build Your Word Power" quizzes in *Reader's Digest;* "Dear Abby," horoscopes, and "Hints from Heloise" (save your old onion bags and use them for hairnets!) in the newspaper.

Until second grade. That's when I finally got a real book to read.

■ ■ ■ ■

My cousin Gloria-Jean — a year older, dark curly haired to my straight blond — went to Maisie E. Quinn, the new elementary school in town. Like us, our schools were physically opposites: hers a rambling one-story with lots of windows; mine, painted yellow with shiny wood floors and old enough that our grandmother and parents had gone there. Maisie E. Quinn had a cafeteria; we ate our brown-bag lunches at our desks. And Maisie E. Quinn had a library.

That is where, I suppose, my cousin got a copy of and read *Little Women,* and passed it along to me. Until then, the only books I had access to were the ones in the Childhood of Famous Americans series that my second-grade teacher, Miss Virginia Nolan, kept in the back of the classroom. I was working my way through all of those orange-covered books. *John Philip Sousa, Marching Boy. Betsy Ross, Girl of Old Philadelphia. Eli Whitney, Boy Mechanic. Little Women* was something else. Fat, with small type and many chapters, it was a real book, the kind I glimpsed when my mother pulled me past the tiny Books department at Ann & Hope, the local discount store. The kind I imagined filled shelves in libraries.

From the first line — " 'Christmas won't be Christmas without any presents,' grumbled Jo, lying on the rug" — I was hooked. With each detail — the introduction of the four March sisters, the utterance of that beloved nickname "Marmie" for their mother, the absent father away at war, the plays written and performed by the March sisters, the neighbor boy Laurie — I fell deeper and deeper into the story. All these years later I recognize how magical this experience truly was. I wanted to live inside a book, and this was the first time I really did.

"I'm going to call you Marmie," I told my mother, surely clutching *Little Women* because I did not put that book down.

"What? No. No, you're not," my no-nonsense mother said.

A day later: "May I carry a baked potato to keep my hands warm? And put it inside a muff?" I asked.

"No! Put on your mittens!" Then with a sigh: "Why are you so weird?"

She had dreamed of a beauty-queen daughter, a cheerleader, a popular girl. Instead she got me, a pageant dropout after just two trophies, too clumsy to be a cheerleader or playground star, quoting "Drama in Real Life" and wondering aloud about photosynthesis.

Little Women's pages brought me into a different world from my Italian immigrant one, which was large and loving, dramatic and loud. Our house was always full of relatives, many of whom spoke very little

English. We were taught to respect our elders, which meant to kiss them hello and goodbye. Even though this often earned me a few dollars from grateful relatives who pinched my cheek or stroked my blond banana curls, cooing, *Bella!*, I didn't like the way they smelled (I realize now that they smelled of food cooking, chopped onions and garlic, dirt and sun). I didn't like that we kids were required to give up our seats to them and crowd together on the sofa or floor, silent.

My great-grandmother, Nonna, was a strong, imposing woman, a *strega* who cured sciatica, migraines, and broken hearts through prayers and magic. People lined up on our block for her services, offering embroidered linens, homemade wine, and the best eggplants and squash from their gardens in lieu of money. Still, Nonna was afraid of two things: flush toilets because she believed they could flush you away, and furnaces because she thought at night they released toxic fumes. Luckily, we did have a toilet, though Nonna kept an outhouse in the backyard, a huge source of embarrassment for me. However she refused to get a furnace. Instead we had a coal stove in the kitchen until 1966. The coal man came every week, and Mama Rose and Nonna shoveled the coal into the coal bin in the dirt basement and started the fire in the kitchen stove early on cold winter mornings.

They also grew much of the food we ate. The community garden stretched far behind our house, and from it came the tomatoes and peppers and cucumbers and string beans; the cherries and pears and apples and figs; the zucchini and mint and basil and carrots. They raised chickens and rabbits too, and before I left for school I was sent into the backyard to kiss them goodbye, gagging at their blood-spattered aprons and the feathers and fur that lay on the ground at their feet.

Little Women took me away from all of this and transported me to the March household in Massachusetts during the Civil War. It was all I could think about at school:

What will Jo do when Amy burns her manuscript? Will Laurie join the sisters' club, the Pick-wick Club? What will happen next? As soon as I got home, Mama Rose would hand me a plate of bread covered in spaghetti sauce or a handful of figs, and I'd sit eating and reading until it was time to set the table for dinner. Some afternoons I would look up, surprised by the shift of light in the room. Surprised that I was actually still in the kitchen rocking chair at home in my little town, that my brother was at the table with his slide ruler and math book, that dinner was ready.

Then I reached chapter 36: "Beth's Secret." Beth is the most lovable, kindest March sister. Jo is confident and ambitious, Meg maternal and ordinary, Amy pretty and spoiled. But Beth! So sweet! So frail after an earlier illness. All fall she appeared to be melancholy, and now in chapter 36 she confesses to Jo that was because she knew she would die soon. Although Jo tries to convince her otherwise, Beth insists it's true. To my seven-year-old self, the idea that a beloved character might die was almost too much to bear. But the idea that we somehow know when we are going to die was downright terrifying. Had my mother's sister Ann — my namesake — known that when she went into the hospital to get her wisdom teeth pulled, she was going to die? Then why had she gone?

Why didn't she cancel the operation and stay home? Had her brother, my uncle Brownie, known he'd have a fatal heart attack at a dance on Valentine's night? But why wouldn't he go straight to the hospital instead?

For several chapters, Beth goes virtually unmentioned, which lulled me into a false sense of security. See? She wasn't going to die! Would Amy and Laurie dance together in Nice if Louisa May Alcott intended to kill off Beth? Would Meg and John work so hard on their marriage if doom was around the corner? Would Jo throw herself into writing for the *Weekly Volcano* if her favorite sister were about to die? Would a writer dedicate so many chapters to illustrating the pros and cons of marriage — Meg and John's, yes, but also Jo's decision to say no to Laurie's proposal — if a main character was dying? I decided no. Beth would surely live.

As an adult, and a writer, I suspect that Beth *had* to die. Her role in the second half of the novel did not seem tenable. Elizabeth Lennox Keyser posits that Beth's quiet, old-fashioned character who clings to outdated values symbolizes the changing role of women and therefore had to die. Still, when I began chapter 40: "The Valley of the Shadow" at the breakfast table one morning and read about the family setting up a special room for Beth with her piano and Amy's drawings in it, an overwhelming dread filled me.

I tucked the book into my pile of textbooks and walked to school, that dread growing with each step. At school, I hung my red wool jacket with the toggle buttons on a hook in the hallway and took my seat in the back of the room, *Little Women* open in my lap. Meg was bringing the twins to visit Beth, almost like a farewell. I swallowed hard, afraid I might start to cry. I kept reading.

Our mornings began when Miss Nolan entered the classroom and all forty of us jumped to our feet.

"Good morning, class," Miss Nolan would say.

"Good morning, Miss Nolan,"

we'd reply.

We'd pivot to face the flag, bend our heads for a moment of silence, then place our hands over our hearts and recite the Pledge of Allegiance. After which Miss Nolan would announce the name of the patriotic song we'd sing — "America the Beautiful" or "God Bless America" or, my favorite, "The Battle Hymn of the Republic." Miss Nolan would then make a downward motion with her hands and we'd sit.

But on the day Beth was dying, I didn't hear Miss Nolan enter the classroom. I wasn't aware of the class rising, or saying the Pledge of Allegiance, or singing a patriotic song. While all of that went on around me, Beth peacefully died. Just like that. When the class took their seats again, I looked up, stunned by grief.

Miss Nolan was looking right at me.

"Ann," she said, "you will stay in for morning recess because you refused to do the morning exercises."

It was the first time I'd ever had to stay in for recess, and if truth be told, that was almost a relief. I was terrible at kickball and jump rope, afraid of the monkey bars, and as a mostly friendless kid never really invited to be part of playground activities. When I wasn't playing jacks, I sat alone and made up stories in my head. It was also the first time I'd ever gotten into trouble, and I worried about what else it might mean. What if Miss Nolan made my mother leave work and come to school? What if she sent me home? I couldn't concentrate on anything but the big hand on the clock dropping into place at 10:10, when the bell would ring and send everyone, two by two, into the playground.

Finally, 10:10 came, the big hand on the clock clicking noisily into place. The bell rang. The class filed out. And Miss Nolan, sitting regally at her desk, beckoned me forward. Clutching *Little Women,* I made my slow way up the aisle to her. So terrified was I that I still remember that I was wearing a pink-and-white polka-dot dress that day, and that I held the heavy book to my chest.

Miss Nolan turned her rheumy blue eyes toward me.

"Why didn't you do the morning exercises?" she asked me. "What were you doing?"

I opened my mouth to answer, but I couldn't put into words the enormity of the effect this book had on me, how I could think of nothing else, how I reread sentences out loud just for the magic of them.

Finally, I held *Little Women* out in front of me and managed to sputter, "Beth *died.*" Having said it out loud, I burst into tears and dropped to the ground with grief.

At first, Miss Nolan looked bewildered. But quickly she ordered me to get up.

"You're reading *Little Women*?" she asked, looking at the book in my hands.

Unable to muster any more words, I nodded.

"And you understand it?" she asked.

Again, I nodded.

Miss Nolan considered this for what seemed a very long time. Then she asked me to tell her what the book was about.

At this, I began to talk — about Marmie and the March sisters and the plays they put on, about Laurie next door and vain Amy and Jo who wanted to be a writer and how Beth died. I told her it was about family but also about war and dreams and writing and . . . "And," I said, "everything. It's about everything."

Now it was Miss Nolan who nodded. She paused, then pointed to the books — Childhood of Famous Americans — that lined the bookshelves in the back of the classroom.

"I don't want you to go out to recess anymore," she said. "I want you to stay inside and read all those books."

And I did. I read every one. Then Miss Nolan gave me all the third-grade books, and I read every one of them too. By the time I left her class, I'd finished half of the fourth-grade books as well.

How can I describe what reading gave to me? An escape from my lonely school days, where girls seemed to speak a language I didn't understand. A glimpse into the possibilities of words and stories. A curiosity about the world and about people — the young Amelia Earhart seeing her first airplane, Helen Keller's silent world, Nancy Drew solving mysteries, David Copperfield surviving the streets of Victorian London.

My parents learned about life from hardship. My mother lost her father when she was only sixteen. She had to drop out of high school, where she was the social committee chairman and a star softball player, and go to work in factories:

bleaching linens, making artificial flowers, attaching snaps to American Tourister luggage. My father dropped out of school too, to escape poverty in rural Indiana. He joined the navy, and by traveling around the world learned how to eat in a restaurant, what kind of cocktail to order, how to tie a tie and polish his shoes. They married young — she was nineteen and he was twenty-one — and grew up together, learning how to raise babies and cook dinner and save money and build a home.

Me? I learned from books.

For as long as I can remember, I wanted something big, something I could not name. I did not know what it was, only what it wasn't. It wasn't in my small hometown. It wasn't nine-to-five, or ordinary, or anything I had ever seen before. I would sit on the landing at the top of the stairs at home and look out the little window at Aunt Julia and Uncle Joe's house across the street. *Someday I will go beyond there,* I would think. I'd look at the rooftop of Auntie Angie's house. *And beyond there.* Then I'd look at the hill where Auntie Rosie and Uncle Chuckie's houses sat. *And beyond there.* I'd focus on a distant point, and think: *Someday I'll even go beyond there.*

This was in the late '60s and early '70s. I'd grown up with the Vietnam War playing out on television. My brother, Skip, had changed from a boy in raspberry shorts and a matching polo shirt to a long-haired, bearded, cutoff jeans-wearing hippie. Newspapers splashed pictures of student protests, and the Kent State shootings, and marijuana and LSD. The same radio station played the Carpenters' "Close to You" and Crosby, Stills, Nash & Young's "Ohio." In such an upside-down world, how would I get *beyond there*? What did I want? Why did I feel this way? What did I believe?

In 1967, when I was ten years old, our town finally got a library.

I went there twice a week, walking past the children's section and heading right for adult fiction.

I can still remember craning my

neck to look at all those beautiful books. I whispered the writers' names: Evan Hunter, Victor Hugo, Harold Robbins, Herman Wouk, Fred Mustard Stewart, Dashiell Hammett, Edith Wharton, Dorothy Parker. So many books! At random I pulled one from the shelf. And then another. I filled my arms with books.

And I read.

I read about small-town gossip in *Peyton Place* and inner-city schools in *The Blackboard Jungle;* I read about Hollywood in *Valley of the Dolls* and a horrific crime in *In Cold Blood.* In that library I was handed a blueprint on how to live the mysterious, unnamable, big dream life I wanted. I was handed books.

And through reading them, I grew up to find that very life.

LESSON 1: HOW TO DREAM

MARJORIE MORNINGSTAR

BY HERMAN WOUK

When *Marjorie Morningstar* was published in 1955, *Time* magazine referred to it as "an outmoded adolescent cliché." *Kirkus Review* wrote: "It is the kind of book women — just past the age of illusion — will read with absorbed interest, occasional ironic recognition, and ultimate critical detachment. But — despite the ease with which the story can be criticized, it will be read." And read it was. *Marjorie Morningstar* sold more copies

43

than *Gone with the Wind,* and in 1958 it was made into a movie starring Natalie Wood as Marjorie.

But as a teenager, I chose the books I read not by reviews or jacket copy or book sales. No, I chose by heft. I loved nothing more than the weight of a heavy book in my arms as I moved through the school hallways. In study hall, my homework finished, I fell into a fat novel that seemed to never end. That I didn't want to end. Halfway through a seven-hundred-page book, hundreds of pages still waited for me. *Doctor Zhivago. Les Misérables.* James Michener's *Hawaii.* Anything by Harold Robbins. I read indiscriminately. Highbrow. Lowbrow. Without any guidance from the librarians in my small mill town in Rhode Island. Their job seemed to be just to stamp due dates in the back of the books, not to recommend them. It was with this lack of direction, this love of novels the weight of cement, that I came upon *Marjorie Morningstar.*

I first read Herman Wouk's novel in 1972, when I was fifteen years old. And I have reread it almost every year since. As an adult, I saw the similarities between the Morgensterns and my own family. Marjorie's father had come to the United States at the age of fifteen, *"a fleck of foam on the great wave of immigration from Eastern Europe."* I lived with a dizzying array of Italian immigrant relatives. In the novel, Mr. Morgenstern owned the Arnold Importing Company, *"a well-known dealer in feathers, straws, and other materials for ladies' hats."* Like my own father, who commuted several hours every day to his job in Government Center in Boston so that we could rise above our blue-collar immigrant roots, Wouk writes of Mr. Morgenstern: *"Every year since his marriage he had spent every dollar he earned on the comfort of his family and the improvement of their station in life."* And like Marjorie, who understood her father's sacrifices — *"her parents had done much to make up for their immigrant origin. She was grateful to them for this, and proud of them."* — I too took pride in how

my parents, two high-school drop-
outs who'd married before they
were old enough to vote, had
bought our family a slice of the
American Dream: two cars, family
vacations, T-bone steaks on the
grill, and Tanqueray and Johnnie
Walker in the liquor cabinet.

But at fifteen, that first time I read
the novel, I thought that Herman
Wouk had somehow climbed into
my brain and emerged with my
story. *I* was Marjorie Morningstar.
Slightly spoiled. Boy crazy. Curious
about sex. Terrified of sex. Raised
by prudish, old-school parents.
Although we lived far from Manhattan and an apartment on Cen-
tral Park West, my life seemed a
mirror image of Marjorie's. West

Warwick, Rhode Island, my small hometown, was once famous for Fruit of the Loom manufacturing and a bustling main street with two fancy women's clothing stores and a men's shop that sold expensive suits. But by the time I was a teenager, the shops and mills were mostly boarded up and the Pawtuxet River, which had helped those factories run, was polluted. The one factory that still operated made soap, and that was the smell that filled the air on hot afternoons. At Christmas, they opened their doors and sold Jade East soap on a rope at discount prices.

My immigrant great-grandparents left Italy in the late 1800s to work in the great Natick Mill, buying a house right up the hill from it. The Natick Mill burned down in 1941, the summer before my mother turned ten. But her family stayed put, working in factories around the state. I grew up in the house my great-grandparents bought when they arrived in the United States, where my grandmother married and had ten children, where my mother at the age of eighty-five still lives. The house is small, just three bedrooms with sloping ceilings upstairs and one bathroom downstairs.

As I've said, as a teenager I would sit at the top of the stairs, staring out the tiny window there. I could see the rooftops of three of my aunts' houses. I could see a distant water tank. On a clear day I could see all the way to the next town. *Someday,* I would think, *I'll even go beyond there.* Just thinking this would thrill me. Deep inside, I had a gnawing, a yearning, for something I could not name. All I knew was that I wouldn't find it in West Warwick, or even in Rhode Island. It was *beyond there.* Despite my parents' warnings, I threw myself into the path of everything that might take me *beyond there.* At fourteen, I became a Marsha Jordan Girl, one of eight teen models for Jordan Marsh, the fancy Boston department store that had opened a branch at our new mall. That job took me all over New England. My friend Beth and I went by bus and train alone to modeling jobs, landing spots in fashion shows for *Brides* magazine and *Mademoiselle.* With the money I earned, I took vacations to Bermuda and the Bahamas before I finished high school.

But that wasn't enough for me. As a junior I tried out for and won the coveted role as teen editor from Rhode Island for *Seventeen* magazine. I wrote dispatches from Rhode Island on fashion, pop culture, and trends. At the end of my yearlong tenure, I won a Best Teen Editor Award, which gave me another year at *Seventeen* and a heavy silver charm with their logo on it. All of these things were somehow going to get me wherever it was I was trying to go. And this yearning I felt was the same one that Herman Wouk expressed so perfectly in the character of Marjorie Morningstar.

Marjorie defies her parents by taking a job as an actress in a summer stock company in the Catskills. And then she defies them even more when she falls in love with and begins a sexual relationship with the director, Noel Airman. What is evident to everyone — her fellow drama club friends at Hunter College, the other summer stock actors, and Marjorie herself — is that she is special, talented, destined for great things. Before she meets Noel, Marjorie dates many boys, all of them worthy suitors.

She enjoys teasing them, flirting, kissing. But her traditional Jewish parents warn her about the dangers of sex, warnings that she holds dear until the summer she's nineteen.

Marjorie falls for Noel the summer before, but he is involved with another actress. That winter, she goes downtown to Bank Street to stand *"across the street from the shabby red brick house where he lived, staring at the windows, while snow caked her beaver coat and caught in her eyelashes."* I read this as if I'd made a great discovery. I sighed. I read the passage again, out loud. I remember where I was — on my bed with its yellow-and-white checked bedspread — and what I wore — my faded Levi's and red peasant blouse. In my doorway hung long strands of colorful beads that I'd spent months stringing; taped to one wall was a Jules Feiffer dancer cartoon; on the stereo Simon and Garfunkel sang "The Dangling Conversation." That song spoke to my yearning too, to my desire for a love in which *"you read your Emily Dickinson, and I my Robert Frost . . ."*

Why did Marjorie standing on a snowy street staring at the apartment where the man she loved lived so affect me? Perhaps because sometimes at night I sat in my parents' Chevy in front of Peter Hayhurst's house — he who had broken my tender heart — hoping for a glimpse of him? Perhaps because as she longed for Noel, Marjorie let Wally Wronken court her, just as I let boys take me to the movies and kiss me in their convertibles while I longed for Peter Hayhurst? Perhaps because Marjorie's romanticism, bravery, idealism, and foolishness were just like mine? Marjorie Morningstar knew me. She *was* me, and I was her.

The light outside had dimmed as I sat reading, and I leaned over to turn on the light by my bed. In the very next chapter, Marjorie goes on dates with dull boys and walks alone on Riverside Drive, mooning for Noel. *"The soft April air blowing across the blue river, the smell of the blossoming cherry and crab-apple trees, the swaying of their bunched pink branches, filled her with bitter-sweet melancholy. Often she would slip a book of poetry in her pocket, and would drop on a bench, after walking far, to read Byron or Shelley or Keats."* I remember having to put the book down. I remember crying, filled with my own teenage bittersweet melancholy. Like Marjorie, I dated dull boys who tried hard to impress me, buying me steaks at Valle's Steak House or taking me dancing at the Ocean View by the beach. I too took long solo walks — not on a city street, but on the beach — and sat in the salty air to read Emily Dickinson and Robert Frost, Allen Ginsberg and Rod McKuen.

When I composed myself, I

picked up the book again. Wally Wronken appears at the Morgensterns' apartment to invite Marjorie to accompany him to the Cloisters in a rainstorm. After the rain stops, he leads her *"around a corner of thick bushes into a curving shadowy path filled with a curious lavender light."* He has led her onto an avenue *"solidly arched and walled with blooming lilacs."* With water dripping on her upturned face, Marjorie takes Wally's hand. *"She was not sure what was rain and what was tears on her face. She wanted to look up at lilacs and rolling white clouds and patchy blue sky forever . . ."* *Yes!* my brain, my heart shouted. *That's what I want too!* So moved by this is Marjorie that she looks at ugly, young, pathetic Wally and kisses him on the mouth. *"They were holding each other's hands, and raindrops were dripping on them from the lilacs."* *"I'm going to plant lilac lanes all over town,"* Wally tells her in a hoarse voice. But Marjorie is already done with him. *"It's fading,"* she tells Wally. *"It's becoming just a lane of lilacs."* Still, she promises him there will be another kiss only when they find such lilacs again.

Somehow, that yearning I felt was taking shape as I read *Marjorie Morningstar.* I wanted a man like Noel Airman. I wanted to move away from home and defy my prudish Catholic parents and have sex with a man I loved. But I wanted the kiss under the lilacs too. That kiss and those lilacs seemed enormously important to me, even though less than a hundred pages later, when Wally and Marjorie see each other at South Wind the next summer, she doesn't remember them.

What I understood when I read *Marjorie Morningstar* as an adult is that of course Noel Airman will break Marjorie's heart and destroy her dreams. *"I eat little girls like you,"* he tells her. Then he does just that. But as a young girl, I held my breath as I followed every twist and turn of their affair. I felt the sharp pangs of heartbreak along with her, recalling how Peter Hayhurst broke my own fragile heart.

But it is the final nine pages of the novel, written in the form of Wally Wronken's diary, that truly break my heart every time. Marjorie gave up on her acting career, married a lawyer, and moved to Westchester. Marjorie Morningstar became Marjorie Schwartz, suburban wife and mother. Critics argue that Wouk is suggesting that Marjorie is lucky: she has had sex with another man, yet still marries a nice Jewish doctor. Perhaps, some critics contend, Wouk is telling readers that sex and rebellion and striving aren't as great as young women hope they will be.

As a young woman back then and today as a middle-aged woman, those last nine pages slay me because Marjorie has let me down. *"And if she wasn't the bright angel I thought, she was a lovely girl,"* Wally tells us. *"And where is that girl now? She doesn't even remember herself as she was."* Wally acknowledges his own loss in Marjorie Morningstar becoming Marjorie Schwartz: he will never have that second kiss under the lilacs. *"Yet how beautiful she was! She rises up before me as I write . . . her face wet with rain, nineteen years old, in my arms and yet maddeningly beyond my reach . . ."*

What I know now looking back at that girl on the bed with the yellow-and-white checked bedspread in the sad mill town, is that *Marjorie Morningstar* moved her so much not just because she saw herself in Marjorie and her family in the Morgensterns. No, *Marjorie Morningstar* gave her — me — the passion to never forget the bright angel who wanted everything, all of it, to go *out there,* wherever that might be. What I decided, what I knew in the deepest parts of me as I read those final pages through tears that wouldn't stop, was that I would, in the final analysis, not be anything like Marjorie at all.

Maybe that's why I reread it every year. Maybe, as time beats me up and grief or loneliness or a new kind of bittersweet melancholy take hold, I need to remind myself to keep going, keep reaching, to not forget the girl who believed she could have everything and anything at all. Maybe even now I am still waiting for that metaphorical kiss under the lilacs. Maybe I always will.

Lesson 2: How to Become a Writer

THE BELL JAR

BY SYLVIA PLATH

It was the summer I spent stringing yards of beads to make that
curtain for the doorway to my
bedroom. I did other things that
summer, of course. I rode the waves
at East Beach and Scarborough,
slathered Coppertone on my long
skinny body, lay under the hot sun
with lemon juice in my hair and
sand in my bikini bottom. I learned
to play Frisbee. The boy who taught
me was a college boy, nineteen

years old, a friend of my brother Skip's. I was only fourteen, and to sit beside that older boy in his white V W Bug was one of my greatest pleasures. That summer, he took me to movies I didn't fully understand. *Getting Straight* with Elliott Gould and *Carnal Knowledge* with — surprisingly to me — Art Garfunkel, whose angelic voice sang some of my favorite songs from my record player — "The Sound of Silence" and "April Come She Will" and "Kathy's Song" and "Bridge over Troubled Water."

Those beads.

Where did I get them, that summer of 1971? Too young to drive, stuck in a town with a main street of boarded-up stores and an X-rated movie theater and dark bars, somehow I acquired enough beads to fill a doorway. I remember the oblong garnet ones, the round amber and the clear teardrops, the midnight blue and cobalt blue, the tiny silver. Although I remember them as glass — the way they sparkled as I strung them in my backyard under the sun! — surely they must have been made of plastic. So many beads! I kept them on a cookie sheet (though in my household cookie sheets were called pizza pans) so that I could better see them, the sizes and shapes and colors, and decide in what order I should string them.

My bedroom was girlish — white

furniture trimmed in gold, yellow-and-white gingham bedspread with matching curtains, a frilly bedside lamp — and I suppose that beaded doorway was meant to show who I really was, or who I was trying to become. A girl who didn't match, someone exotic and mysterious and deep. I would lie on that gingham-covered bed and play "The Dangling Conversation" and I would yearn for a boy who knew who Frost and Dickinson were, who would read beside me, who would understand this peculiar person I was. I would play "I Am a Rock" and I would cry as Simon and Garfunkel sang: *I have my books, and my poetry to protect me . . .*

I had nothing at all to be depressed about, or even to cry about. My parents adored me. Skip — five years older than me — had finally stopped farting in my face and turning his eyelids inside out to scare me; and after years as a lonely, alienated child, adolescence had brought me friends and slumber parties and all the giggling and inside jokes I needed. Still, a rock of sadness settled in my gut, immovable and heavy. When my ninth-grade English teacher taught us about haikus and then set us free to write our own, I wrote: *Waves wash away sand / Just as He washes away / The life we cherish.* "Is Ann depressed?" the teacher asked my mother in an emergency conference. "No," my mother said, "she's just weird."

That weirdness seemed to grow stronger with puberty. Insomnia hit, and at night beneath my gingham bedspread I'd watch Johnny Carson and then Tom Snyder on my tiny portable black-and-white television. After Snyder, TV ended, and I would read until my eyes drooped. But once I turned off the light and got on my side, panic gripped me. My heart raced and I'd sit up, turning the light back on, almost certain I would find something there. What that something might be, I can't say. We were a family that believed in ghosts, and often at breakfast we reported sightings: mysterious bruises on my father's arms came from a ghost pinching him; the dip of the bed beside my mother was a ghost sitting next to her; the soft breeze my grandmother felt even though the windows were closed tight meant a ghost had kissed her. Perhaps I was expecting to find my dead great-grandmother or aunt in the room, but the fear felt bigger than even ghosts.

When my mother called out to me and asked what was wrong, I could never name it. "Nothing!" I would say. *Everything,* I would think. Many nights she got dressed and drove me to the Dunkin' Donuts down the street, where we'd sit in a booth and drink coffee and eat glazed doughnuts until I'd calmed down. It didn't occur to me until I was an adult how difficult those forays into the night must have been for her — she had to be at work at the candy factory by seven the next morning. By the time I emerged from my grateful sleep for school, she was long gone.

The summer of the beads, I read *The Bell Jar.* I remember the cover. A pink so pale it almost looked white. The black letters with their curlicued *T* and *B* and *J.* The red rose stretched across the edge. Unaware as I was of things like book reviews, I didn't know that the book I'd plucked from the library shelf was a new one, just published in the United States. I didn't even know — though surely this was in the author's bio — that Sylvia Plath had committed suicide on February 11, 1963, just a few weeks after *The Bell Jar* had been published by Harper & Row in Britain under the pseudonym Victoria Lucas. After her death, her estranged husband, poet Ted Hughes, promised her mother, Aurelia Plath, that the novel wouldn't be published in the United States during her lifetime. But the wild success of Sylvia Plath's poetry collection *Ariel* and the rumors that Victoria Lucas was indeed Plath, made the demand for *The Bell Jar* in the United States huge. Bookstores in New York City sold bootleg British copies of the novel, but it wasn't until an editor at Random

House learned that it was no longer eligible for copyright protection, thereby forcing Harper's hand, that *The Bell Jar* was finally published here, despite Hughes's promise.

An immediate bestseller, Plath's story of beautiful, brilliant Esther Greenwood's breakdown spoke to my generation. The minds of women were just being discussed openly as feminism soared. Questions of career, sex, marriage, and finding yourself were, I suspect, what kept me up at night. In my small town, only a handful of graduating seniors went on to college. People who were born in West Warwick tended to stay in West Warwick. But I wanted to leave. For what I cannot say, nor could I say then.

I wanted to be a writer — in fact, *was* a writer in many ways, filling purple notebooks with poems and stories and short plays — and imagined a writer's life, perhaps in Greenwich Village or Paris. Certainly there were no writers in my town, or as far as I knew, in all of Rhode Island. When my ninth-grade guidance counselor asked me what I wanted to do with my life, I told him I wanted to be a writer. Mr. Stone, in his brown corduroy suit and tinted aviator glasses, shook his head sadly. "Ann," he said, "people don't do that."

My eyes drifted to the shelves against the wall. "Then how do we get all these books?" I asked him.

Mr. Stone glanced at the books for a moment, then told me, "All those writers are dead."

He was right, of course. This was, after all, 1969 or '70 and we only read the dead white guys. Would I write in anonymity, I wondered, and have my stories published only after I died?

By then, our library had opened at last. I read every book I could get my hands on. And I had just read a paperback called *How to Become an Airline Stewardess* by Kathryn Cason. *For that special breed of young women with their eyes on the stars — and their hearts set on a jet-paced career with wings!* the cover proclaimed. Inside were promises of breakfast in New York, lunch in Bermuda, dinner in Rome, and boyfriends in every city in the world.

"Then I'd like to be an airline stewardess," I told Mr. Stone.

He shook his head again. "Ann, smart girls do not become airline stewardesses. You should be a teacher or a secretary or make your life nice and easy and get married."

I don't know how I replied to his suggestions, but I know that I dismissed them. I didn't want to be any of those things — teacher, secretary, wife. But unable to name this yearning I had for something different, all I knew was that I wanted to get out of West Warwick. Writers, I thought, needed adventures. Airline stewardesses had adventures. If my ticket out was on a jet, then I would take it. Those adventures would give me ideas for the novels I would write. The next time I went to the library, I checked out *How to Become an Airline Stewardess* again, and dutifully recorded the qualifications (height! weight!) and the interview tips (don't wear a turtleneck!) in one of my purple notebooks. I would see the world, I decided. I would run with the bulls and jump naked in fountains in Paris. And then someday, somehow, I would be a writer.

The Bell Jar seemed to be written just for me. Esther Greenwood wanted to be a writer too. She had won a fashion magazine contest that sent her and eleven other girls to New York City for a month with all their expenses paid and *"piles and piles of free bonuses, like ballet tickets and passes to fashion shows and hair stylings at a famous salon . . ."* Esther had the same doubts I had. *"How could I write about life when I'd never had a love affair or a baby or even seen anybody die?"* Esther wonders. She remembers a girl who won a prize for a short story about pygmies in Africa and asks: *How could I compete with that sort of thing?*

Despite the perfect boyfriend, Buddy, who wants to marry her, Esther doesn't want to get married. She's curious about sex, but doubtful about matrimony. She worries that once someone liked her, he would *"sink into ordinariness,"* that she would find fault after fault with him like she did with Buddy. Esther Greenwood was the first character I met who expressed the very things I worried over as "I Am a Rock" played again and again on my record player. I worried over ordinariness — mine in particular. I worried over the idea of getting married and staying in my hometown forever. I worried over that thing I wanted that no one could help me name or find. No one except Esther. *"The last thing I wanted was infinite security and to be the place an arrow shoots off from,"* she says to explain why she doesn't want to get married. *"I wanted change and excitement and to shoot off in all directions myself, like the colored arrows from a Fourth of July rocket."*

Around me, my older cousins got married at our church, Sacred Heart. The brides wore flowing white gowns embellished with tiny pearls and lace, long veils, bouquets of lilies; the grooms wore tuxedos and shiny shoes, boutonnieres and clean-shaven faces. There were bridesmaids, in mauve velvet or pale yellow jersey knit and dyed-to-match shoes, clutching chrysanthemums or daisies; groomsmen in too-tight rented tuxedos, their shirts the color of those dresses. At the reception at the Club 400, whiskey sours flowed from fountains, the Champagne toast was pink and sweet, and we ate ziti, chicken stuffed with rice, green beans amandine, and iceberg lettuce topped with a wedge of tomato.

The couple moved into an apartment, then bought a small house. They had a baby, then another baby. On Sundays they came to our house and visited Mama Rose and ate lasagna and threw barbs at each other. He complained that she never let him have fun. She complained that he didn't talk to her enough. They stared out at us blankly, their faces as bland as bologna. I remembered Buddy Willard telling Esther that after she had children she wouldn't want to write poems anymore. Esther compared being married to being brainwashed: *"afterward you went about numb as a slave in some private totalitarian state,"* she said. I watched my cousins and knew Esther was, once again, right.

And then, there was madness itself. Didn't I sometimes feel out of control? And other times paralyzed? Like Esther, I worked hard all my life to get A's, worried over each test and research paper, studied and studied and studied. But wasn't that need to get those A's part of what drove her mad? Esther obsessed about the Rosenbergs; I obsessed about Charlie Manson and Richard Speck. If Esther Greenwood with her scholarship to

a good college, her adoring boyfriend, her good grades and writing
talent, could go mad, then couldn't
anybody? Couldn't I?

As that summer came to an end, I
hung those beads in my doorway.
My parents, ever practical, ever
befuddled by my strange desires,
refused to remove the door to my
room, so I pushed it open and held
it that way with a heavy iron door-
stop. The beads made a glistening
curtain that whispered when I
walked through it. They looked
exotic, sophisticated, important.

As we always did before school
started, my cousin and I took the
bus from the bottom of the hill to
downtown Providence. Downcity,

it was called. The bus cost thirty-five cents and made one stop: at the state mental hospital. Maybe reading *The Bell Jar* added to my fascination with that place, which looked almost like a college campus with its curving walkways, large leafy trees, and small groupings of brick buildings — except the windows in those buildings had bars on them. I didn't know then that the hospital where Esther Greenwood went was a private one, surely more lovely than the one I saw outside the bus window. I didn't know such differences even existed. Onto the bus stepped a handful of patients: a man who mumbled to himself, a blank-eyed woman led by a nurse, a woman with an angry

face who periodically shouted ob-
scenities, and — most fascinating
to me — a woman with her hair
dyed bright red, her lips smeared
with hot-pink lipstick, her entire
eyelids painted baby blue, her
cheeks overly powdered and
rouged. She wore multiple shiny
necklaces and a Kelly-green dress.
I thought she looked like human
neon. Someone behind me whispered, "Crazy," as the woman regally walked down the aisle to an
empty seat. I thought of Esther sitting in the Boston Public Garden
reading a scandal sheet of stories
about murders and robberies and
suicides, or sitting all day on a
beach in a skirt and high heels
fingering a box of razor blades. I

thought of myself sobbing over "The Dangling Conversation," or pacing in the middle of the night, how things felt so enormous to me, so vital. What was the difference between Esther and me? This woman and me?

In Providence, at the department stores Shepard's and Gladdings, my cousin and I tried on clothes in front of triple mirrors that multiplied our reflections over and over, a strange effect that always fascinated me. We went to Alexander's for lunch, a restaurant with white tablecloths and Salisbury steak. We felt so grown-up with our shopping bags crowded into the red booth eating our fancy food. In one of those bags was my first-day-of-school outfit: mauve hot pants with a matching vest that came below my knees and a flowered puckered shirt.

Weeks later, in that very outfit, I was walking through Jordan Marsh into the mall when a woman sitting at a table at the entrance stopped me. "Have you ever thought about modeling?" she asked me. I said yes, though I hadn't thought about it at all. She invited me to sit down with her so she could explain about Marsha Jordan Girls. Marsha Jordan Girls were ambassadors for Jordan Marsh, she said. They modeled the clothes in the Juniors department, worked at VIP events here and in Boston (Boston! The very idea gave me shivers!), and represented the store in dozens of ways throughout the year.

"I want to be a Marsha Jordan Girl," I said. It felt like my world had just been blown open, like I was handed a new life, not unlike the one of my vague, big dreams. The woman was explaining that Bonne Bell Cosmetics would come and teach us how to put on makeup, and that we would get special uniforms — she slid a glossy photo of a girl in a gray-and-white pinstriped pantsuit toward me — and have our pictures hanging in the Juniors department. I thought of Esther in New York City, getting hairstyles and clothes, going to fancy lunches. Being a Marsha Jordan Girl sounded similar.

Apparently, lots of girls wanted to be Marsha Jordan Girls, but they only needed eight. I filled out the application eagerly, already imagining a picture of me in that pinstriped suit hanging in the Juniors department. I didn't know that girls had been coming to the store all day to apply, or that I had just had an interview. I only knew that I wanted to be a Marsha Jordan Girl more than anything in the world.

How I longed to *know* things, to be sophisticated and worldly. My father had traveled the globe when he was in the navy, and his stories inspired me to do the same. He told me about eating stuffed dog in Africa and hundred-year eggs in

China; he explained communism and Castro, having lived in both Peking and Guantánamo; he told me to always order name liquor — Heineken, Tanqueray, Johnnie Walker; steak, my father, told me, should always be eaten rare. Yet even all of this advice did not tell me everything I needed to know to leave my working-class upbringing behind.

In *The Bell Jar,* Esther makes social blunders too. When she first arrives at the Amazon hotel in Manhattan, a bellhop carries her suitcase up to her room, then doesn't leave. Instead, he shows her the hot and cold water, how to use the radio, what stations are on the dial, before he finally leaves, slamming the door behind him. *"You ninny,"* her friend Doreen explains later, *"he wanted a tip."* At least a quarter, Doreen continues. Esther can't believe it: *"Now I could have carried that suitcase to my room perfectly well by myself, only the bell hop seemed so eager to do it that I let him. I thought that kind of service came along with what you paid for your hotel room."* When my family traveled, we stayed at motels with swimming pools and ice machines and Magic Fingers on the beds: for a dime the bed shimmied beneath you for a full minute. But I intended someday to stay at fancy hotels in big cities, and then I would tip bellhops, and cabdrivers (Esther quickly learns that they get

91

15 percent of the fare).

When I got home from the mall that afternoon, the phone was already ringing. I was one of sixteen finalists. On Saturday I was to go to the store for a tea. That day was a blur of brownie sundaes, Jordan Marsh executives, and fifteen other smiling girls. Those brownie sundaes were worrisome: a big square brownie, topped with vanilla ice cream, hot fudge, whipped cream, and a cherry, served in a frosty silver goblet. As we ate, the executives and the woman I'd spoken to the other day asked us questions about fashion trends, our favorite subjects in school, and our dreams for the future.

"I want to be a journalist like Barbara Walters," I said, trying not to smear hot fudge on my face or dribble ice cream down my shirt. How could I not think of the scene in which Esther has lunch with her benefactress, Mrs. Guinea, and saw her first fingerbowl? *"The water had some cherry blossoms floating in it, and I thought it must be some clear sort of Japanese after-dinner soup and ate every bit of it, including the crisp little blossoms."* Mrs. Guinea never says anything to Esther, and she muses how it was only later *"when I told a debutante I knew at college about the dinner, that I learned what I had done."* What were the rules for eating a brownie sundae? Should I leave the cherry? To be safe, I did.

In fact, I did not want to be a journalist like Barbara Walters; I wanted to write stories. I have no idea why I said that, except perhaps that teachers and guidance counselors and relatives always laughed when I said I wanted to be a *writer,* to make up stories and publish books. A journalist like Barbara Walters seemed more practical somehow. And the man looked impressed.

By dinnertime the phone rang again. I was a Marsha Jordan Girl.

All these years later, I spend a good amount of my time knitting. I do it to calm myself, to soothe my confused and broken heart, to keep sadness at bay. I do it so that I won't lose my mind. That long-ago summer, when I felt like I was a giant nerve ending exposed to the harsh world, I didn't realize that stringing those long strands of beads in my hot backyard was accomplishing the same thing. That, and reading *The Bell Jar.* The novel was a warning. A possibility. An alternate version of the self I might become. It made me understand that young women did go to New York City and write. It made me glimpse a world of stylish clothes and new hairstyles and independence. It also made me tremble as I glimpsed the other side of a creative soul. How scary our talents and desires can be! How close to the edge we actually live.

LESSON 3: HOW TO ASK WHY

JOHNNY GOT HIS GUN

BY DALTON TRUMBO

"Today in the war," Walter Cronkite said to me every evening from our black-and-white Zenith. Behind him, a map of Southeast Asia, Vietnam divided into north and south, Cambodia and Laos snuggled into it. I barely looked at that map, or the images of soldiers that followed Cronkite's introduction. I played with my favorite doll, Little Miss No Name, an orphan in a burlap patched dress, scraggly blond hair, and one big plastic teardrop on her cheek. Or I cut paper dolls or drew intricate series of stairs on my Etch A Sketch. By junior high, I talked on our heavy black telephone, sitting in front of the television as Cronkite announced the number of dead that day. Artillery fire flashed across the scene. I did my homework, dunked chocolate-covered graham crackers into a glass of milk, wrote haiku in purple ink in my poetry notebook. It had silhouettes of a boy and girl holding hands on a beach. Walter Cronkite said, "Tet Offensive." He said, "Viet Cong. Saigon. Hanoi."

I didn't know why we were fighting in Vietnam. In fact, it was many years later that I learned it all began in 1949, when Mao and communism came to power in China (where my father as a young man in the navy was sent). I knew only the simplest things: Ho Chi Minh was bad, Hanoi was north and Saigon was south, and we had been sending soldiers to fight over there . . . well, to me, forever. The shifting allegiances of the United States, Russia, and France were unknown to me, as was the fact that France had ruled Vietnam — Indochina — and was driven out in 1949. Although I knew that north and Hanoi was communist, I didn't know that the Geneva Accords had established the Seventeenth Parallel as the boundary between Vietnam's Communist north and non-Communist south in 1954, or that the Hanoi regime then resumed war by means of infiltration and southern insurgents. Even though I'm sure Walter Cronkite told me about the assassination of South Vietnam's dictator, Ngo Dinh Diem, in 1963 that led to the bombings and large-scale ground forces under President Johnson, I don't remember these historical details. I just remember watching it: the bombings, the soldiers fighting, the war.

The war ended in 1975, the year after I graduated from high school. I had no childhood without the Vietnam War in it. The draft loomed over everyone's head. At first, there were college deferments. Even so, around the kitchen table my aunts and uncles talked about writing to congressmen or someone — anyone — important. Our family did not know anyone important. But my father had a certain amount of cachet in our relatives' eyes. He had worked for Admiral Rickover at the Pentagon, though only as his driver and assistant. When he retired from the navy after twenty years, he took a job at a company called RMK that shipped goods to Vietnam. The job had required a high security clearance. His boss, Mr. Carothers, adored him. Surely he knew *somebody* who could keep my cousins Stephen, Michael, David, Alfred, and Chip out of the army, out of Vietnam, home and safe.

Stephen enlisted before he could get drafted and spent his time in the army in Walla Walla, Washington. Michael and Alfred got college deferments. But David got drafted and was shipped to Vietnam almost immediately, leaving his fiancée Claudette behind to plan their wedding alone. In my house, Mama Rose lit candles at the feet of statues of saints in the small shrines she kept around — the Virgin Mary, Saint Anthony, Saint Christopher. Novenas were made. I watched the war on TV, emotionless, not once thinking of Cousin David or any of the boys fighting on the screen right in front of me. This was my generation: immune to the horrors of war because it had been playing out in our living room our entire lives. One day our dog barked and growled like crazy outside and we all ran to see what was the matter. Cousin David was making his way up the sidewalk, home again.

Had one year passed? Or two? I have no idea. But the wedding was waiting for him. The bridesmaids had their shoes dyed to match their gowns. The groomsmen rented tuxedos with shirts the same color. At the bridal shower David and Claudette received electric knives and electric can openers and electric toothbrushes. As a girl, I loved weddings, and although I don't remember where this one was to be held, to me then weddings meant those fancy whiskey-sour fountains and string beans amandine and the hard, pale candies the women wrapped in tulle and tied with a ribbon. But just like that, the wedding was called off. David couldn't go through with it. And it seemed to have something to do with what happened in Vietnam. At night great debates roared around the kitchen table. Did they have to return the wedding presents? Did she have to return the engagement ring? Were they breaking up? Or just postponing the wedding?

That was the first indication I had that this war was not a two-dimensional image on my television screen. That gunfire was real. Those bodies falling were people. People dying. A person could go to war in love and return unable to go through with the wedding. Of course, I knew this was true of World War II. All of our fathers, except mine, who was just young enough to miss it, had been in the War. There were lingering bad feelings toward Japan and Germany. We celebrated V-J Day every August — Victory over Japan. We knew who Hitler was (though not the atrocities, not yet), and we knew what had happened on Omaha Beach and Iwo Jima. My cousin's neighbor Frenchie had one arm, the other lost at Iwo Jima. In the eponymous movie about the battle there was a character named Frenchie: him. He was one of the men in the famous statue of soldiers raising the flag. To me — maybe to all of us my age — that was the War. This thing on television was more like the show *Combat!* on Monday nights, Vic Morrow crawling toward the camera in his camouflage, clutching his gun.

The other war — World War I — seemed to have happened a million years earlier. It wasn't until high school that I even learned what had started it, Gavrilo Princip jumping out in front of Archduke Ferdinand in Sarajevo and shooting him and his wife. My father used to tell me about a teacher he had in grade school back in Indiana who was "shell-shocked from the war." If a child tapped his pencil or foot, the teacher would start to shake and run to the closet to hide. I never bothered to ask which war he'd fought in; it wasn't until many years later that I understood it was World War I. In front of the high school in our town stood a statue of a World War I soldier called Jerry, but to me the statue seemed to be there not to commemorate a war but rather to get spray-painted red and white by the Coventry Oakers, our football rivals on Thanksgiving weekend every year. When I watched *All Quiet on the Western Front* on *Saturday Night at the Movies* with Skip and Mama Rose (our parents out playing cards with my aunts and uncles as they did every Saturday night), I didn't even realize the movie was about World War I. World War II was the war that still haunted us, that in many ways seemed more real than the one we were actually fighting at the time.

Although I can't say for certain, I must have gotten a copy of Dalton Trumbo's *Johnny Got His Gun* from one of my brother's friends. They often gave me books to read, most of which I didn't really understand. *The Tin Drum. Siddhartha. The Painted Bird. The Teachings of Don Juan.* But unlike those books, *Johnny Got His Gun* had a profound and lasting impact on me. Originally published in 1939, it is the story of Joe Bonham, an ordinary young man, in love with his sweet-heart back home, who loses his arms, legs, face, ears — after a bomb dropped on him during World War I.

The book I read was a small paperback, and had a black cover with a large white hand forming a peace sign on it. Inside the palm of the hand stands the silhouette of a soldier in the iconic doughboy helmet of World War I, pointing a rifle. It was the edition I read a few years after it was released, dog-eared and wrinkled from so many readings by so many young men facing the draft. *"This was no war for you. This thing wasn't any of your business. What do you care about making the world safe for democ-*

racy? All you wanted to do Joe was live." The little I knew about the Vietnam War sounded eerily similar. The United States was over there fighting for democracy, weren't they? North Vietnam was Communist. Communism was spreading. If they took over South Vietnam, no one was safe from it, were we? *"Oh why the hell did you ever get into this mess anyway? Because it wasn't your fight Joe. You never really knew what the fight was all about."*

Wait, I thought as I read, this was what my brother and his friends were saying in our backyard, on the beach, and sitting around our kitchen table. This wasn't our fight. This wasn't any of our business.

Sometimes I tried to imagine Skip or one of his friends in a uniform, holding a gun, standing in a jungle. I tried to imagine their faces on the soldiers who fought on my television screen every night on the news. But it was too frightening — in the war I watched on TV, the soldiers got shot. They died. I saw coffins draped in American flags, dead boys inside, waiting to come home. It sounds foolish to say this now, but it wasn't until that summer that I realized the war I saw on television was real. Now when Walter Cronkite announced the day's death toll, I listened.

They knew what was important. . . . They died with only one

thought in their minds and that was I want to live I want to live I want to live.

Skip and his friends had college deferments. But still the draft loomed over them. They drank beers and ate Mama Rose's meatballs and sausage and pepper sandwiches and talked about going to Canada or Sweden for amnesty. Although there was something thrilling about that idea — sneaking over a border at night on foot; living among fjords and the Northern Lights — I knew that if you did that you were never allowed home to the United States again. Surely Skip wouldn't opt for that, would he?

They discussed the viability of filing as a conscientious objector. A well-told story in our household was that my mother had dated a conscientious objector during World War II. He was a Quaker and Quakers were against war. (Of course, I had no idea what a Quaker was, except that one peered out at me from our container of oatmeal and that William Penn, founder of Pennsylvania, had been one too.) Was it too late for Skip to convert and become a Quaker? I wondered. After all, our father had converted to Catholicism in order to marry our mother and he always said it was really nothing. "You believe what you believe anyway," he'd say.

All of these conversations made me unsettled in a way I couldn't explain. Suddenly, the war itself made me unsettled. I grew up in a mostly traditional family, surrounded by dozens of relatives who were Democrats, went to town hall meetings, and voted in every election. Two of my uncles had fought in WWII. The other had a bad heart and the army wouldn't take him, but he tried to enlist because you fought for your country. In other words, I was raised a proud American. My father was even born on the Fourth of July. He loved that his birthday was the same day as Independence Day. He'd blast John Philip Sousa music from the minute he woke up, and often at night the men who had come to his party, all of them WWII veterans, picked up broomsticks and mops and marched around the yard with tears in their eyes.

But after I read *Johnny Got His Gun,* I started to question the things I'd been raised to believe. What were we fighting for in Vietnam anyway? Did Americans have the right to tell other countries how to live? What did it even mean to be an American? I started watching the news more carefully, and reading the newspaper reports about the war that I'd been ignoring. I sat in the backyard with Skip and his friends and listened to what they thought, what they believed.

They discussed how Johnson had escalated the war, how we'd killed four hundred civilians at My Lai, how we'd secretly bombed Laos and Cambodia. No one could be trusted, not our president or any of the authority figures in charge.

Johnny thinks of himself as lying like a side of beef for the rest of his life. And for what? *"It was a kind of duty you owed yourself that when anybody said come on son do this or do that you should stand up and say look mister why should I do this for whom am I doing it and what am I going to get out of it in the end?"*

Around me, most of my cousins stayed on the path our parents had set us on. My father used to joke that we just followed our town's main street: baptized at Sacred Heart, wedding at the Club 400, funeral at Prata's Funeral Home. As a child, I had found comfort in our church with its smell of wax and incense, the sounds of shoes walking on marble, the brilliance of its stained-glass windows. I'd loved those weddings at the Club 400 too, the specialness of that whiskey-sour fountain bubbling forth cock-tails the adults caught in special half-moon-shaped glasses.

But asking "Why should I do this?" wasn't just about the war. It was about everything I thought I believed and knew. I'd always had this yearning for something I couldn't name, that no one could help me name. Maybe that yearning was a big question: why?

Something new started taking up airtime on the news. Or maybe it had been happening before I began questioning, became *aware*. But it seemed to me that suddenly college students were protesting the war. They appeared in front of college buildings and on college greens, dozens and dozens of them, long hair and earnest faces, carrying signs: MAKE LOVE NOT WAR and HELL NO WE WON'T GO. They were angry and passionate as they stood shoulder to shoulder, shouting and singing protest songs by Bob Dylan and Peter, Paul, and Mary like "Blowin' in the Wind" and "Where Have All the Flowers

Gone?" I wanted to be one of them, to be a person who cared that much about something, a person who made a difference.

Once again, my world had been cracked open by a book. But this time, the world that was shifting around me — my own small one and the one outside it — and the book itself crashed together in such a way that I felt like I was suddenly awake. Around me, my classmates still seemed unaffected by the war, the demonstrations, all of it. Vietnam had become the backdrop of our childhoods and it was easy to keep it that way, in the background. But I'd had a summer of college boys sitting in my backyard discussing the war. I'd heard them debate my father at our kitchen table and for the first time in my young life I disagreed with him. I'd read *Johnny Got His Gun,* perhaps the greatest antiwar book ever written, a book of which Trumbo himself wrote: "Johnny held a different meaning for three different wars. Its present meaning is what each reader conceives it to be, and each reader is gloriously different from every other reader, and each is also changing. I've let it remain as it was to see what it is."

At school I was labeled a hippie. Even one of my favorite teachers took to calling me Hippie Ann. I wasn't offended; I was proud. To me, being a hippie meant that you cared about the world, that you wanted to help stop the war in Vietnam. With my gypsy skirts and John Lennon round wire-frame glasses, I dressed the part too. Except I wasn't acting; I was a girl too young to really do anything except try to be heard. In 1970, when the Ohio National Guard shot and killed four students at Kent State, I wore a black armband to school for a week. When I watched students on TV protesting the war, I used to think, *Wait for me. Wait for me to grow up enough to join you.*

Of course, the world didn't wait for me to grow up. By the time I went to college, the Vietnam War was finally ending and protests were a thing of the past. The hippies who were still on campus were burnouts who had smoked too much pot or dropped too much acid to do anything meaningful. Those socially minded students had been replaced by boys in white leisure suits and girls practicing the Hustle in their dorm rooms and playing the soundtrack from *Saturday Night Fever.* There were discos instead of sit-ins, high heels instead of sandals. In other words, nothing was how I'd hoped it would be when I arrived at college.

But the events I'd watched take place around me as an adolescent left me someone who leans further left than even my Democratic parents; who still protests and resists war. Although the war of my youth was fought in Vietnam, *Johnny Got His Gun* took place half a century earlier. Reading it didn't just make me take notice of what was happening around me; it showed me the horrors of all wars, of all the dead boys and misguided politicians. It made me ask why then, and it makes me still ask why now.

LESSON 4: HOW TO BUY BOOKS

LOVE STORY

BY ERICH SEGAL

Every week my mother took me along with her to the local discount store, Ann & Hope, where she bought curtains, bath mats, and tablecloths on the cheap. Much to her disapproval, I brought my allowance so that I could buy a Nancy Drew book. The entire series was lined up, yellow spines out, the numbers and titles in order, beginning with *The Secret of the Old Clock* and ending with *The Spider Sapphire Mystery*. I had no

sisters, just a mathematically obsessed brother who solved problems on a slide ruler for fun. But
my cousin Gloria-Jean, a year older
than me, shared my passion for
reading and she also used her allowance to buy a Nancy Drew
book every week. Our plan was to
read every one of them, trading our
newest ones after we'd finished.

At the cash register, my mother
shook her head and sighed. "I cannot believe you are wasting your
money on a book. A book! Of all
things!"

I didn't care. I held that yellow
book close to my chest, and happily handed over my two dollars,
the bills damp and creased.

Along the river of my small town,

mills that had produced textiles in the nineteenth century now stood empty, leaving most of the town unemployed. A Champlin Grant to build a library led to breaking ground behind Main Street, where the movie theater showed XXX movies; Newberry's, the five-and-dime, was boarded up; and sleazy bars replaced what had once been fine clothing stores. To avid readers like Gloria-Jean and me, the progress on the library seemed practically glacial. By the time it finally opened, we had read every Nancy Drew book and were ready to move on.

Move on we did. Agatha Christie and Charles Dickens; Harold Robbins and Herman Wouk; Victor

Hugo and Evan Hunter. We read indiscriminately. We read everything. Three, four, five books a week we read. "A waste of time!" my mother would say when I hung up with Gloria-Jean after chatting about our latest reads. "Put the book down and go outside and play!" In family pictures during this time, I am always holding a book in my lap, my finger holding my place.

Then, in 1970, something almost more miraculous than a library came to town. The Warwick Mall opened, just a mile from my house, an easy walk on a Saturday morning. Boston department stores Jordan Marsh and Filene's anchored each end of the mall. And on the path from one to the other stood the first bookstore I had ever seen. Waldenbooks was a small rectangle tucked between a fast-food steak house and a Spencer's Gifts. Although the lure of a $3.99 steak and a lava lamp were great, nothing called to me more than that bookstore.

At the front, a wooden display showed hardcover bestsellers, face-out. Beside it, a spinning rack held paperbacks, more than I ever imagined existed. Sometimes, I went there and touched every single book, the smell of incense and French fries from the neighboring stores filling my nose, all of it intoxicating.

On one of those visits, the novel

Love Story caught my eye. The book was slender, white, with the title in big red, blue, and green letters. I still remember how Erich Segal's name sat beneath it in red, and how the words *"Love means never having to say you're sorry"* seemed more profound than anything I had ever read. That spring and into fall, *Love Story* remained on the bestseller list, securing its spot on the front display of Waldenbooks. Although I cannot remember how much the book sold for in 1970, I do remember that the price seemed — no, *was* — astronomical to an eighth grader in West Warwick, Rhode Island. If my mother thought spending $1.99 on a Nancy Drew book was a waste of money, what would she say if I brought home this beautiful, expensive hardcover book? I was not a kid who got in trouble, but I could imagine my mother's wrath at such a purchase.

One day, as I stood fondling the book and pondering how love meant never having to say you're sorry, it occurred to me that giving a book to Gloria-Jean would be the most wonderful present anyone had ever given her. Even though we already owned those Nancy Drew books, this book, *Love Story*, was a real book. A hardcover! A bestseller! Imagine owning such a thing! I remember that the cold weather had arrived, and I was wearing my pale blue winter jacket.

Yet I shivered at the thought of it.

I saved my allowance until the December day I could go into Waldenbooks and buy *Love Story,* the first real book I'd ever bought, and the first book I would give as a gift. Could the shaggy-haired, green-eyed boy who rang up the purchase understand how important this moment was for me? I don't think so. After all, he stood behind that cash register all day selling books, as if it were nothing special. Muzak Christmas carols filled the air. Lights twinkled from every storefront. I had never felt the Christmas spirit as much as I did at that moment. But when he asked me if I wanted the book gift-wrapped, I hesitated and shook my head, even though the wrapping paper there was much more beautiful than the kind we had at home from Ann & Hope.

Instead, I tucked the slim book in its Waldenbooks paper bag inside my jacket, and walked home along the snowy streets, past the dilapidated mill houses with their flashing blue Christmas lights, over the bridge that crossed the sluggish Pawtuxet River, past the three churches, and up the big slippery hill. Once inside and warm, I pulled my treasure from the bag. Then I carefully opened the book the tiniest bit, and read it from beginning to end without cracking the spine. I think I began to cry at the first line: *"What can you say about a*

twenty-five-year-old girl who died?"
By the end, when Jenny dies of
leukemia and her young husband,
Oliver, delivers that iconic line —
*"Love means not ever having to say
you're sorry"* — to his wealthy father, I was sobbing.

Certainly I was sobbing because
Jenny died, and because Mr. Bar-
rett had acted so mean to her and
Oliver, and because the father and
son were together again. But looking back on it now, I think too that
this story of a blue-collar girl from
Rhode Island falling in love with a
rich Harvard jock made me —
perhaps for the first time — aware
of deep class differences. In my
town, though there were a few
wealthy families with lawyer or

businessman fathers, most of us were varying degrees of middle class. We were used to the kids, many of them, on welfare; we barely took notice of the kids who couldn't afford rain or snow boots and came to school with Wonder Bread bags tied around their shoes with rubber bands. Jenny and Ollie, I realized, came from two different worlds. And those worlds didn't easily accept each other. What would my place be in this big world I wanted so desperately to see? Through teary eyes, I closed the book and wrapped it in the flimsy Ann & Hope Christmas paper, topping it with a big silver bow.

Since that long-ago day, I have given more books than I can count as Christmas presents. But none have meant as much to me. That first one showed me something I already knew — that owning books is not a waste of money, not at all. But I now realize that it was my first step toward a kind of independence, entering into that world of books and language that was so foreign to my family. But not to me — no, I understood that I would always buy books, that I was a reader and a writer and that to be surrounded by books would always bring me comfort.

This summer, I found myself in the throes of upheaval. Newly divorced, I was leaving my home of almost twenty years, a cozy red Colonial built in 1792, and moving across town with my twelve-year-old daughter Annabelle to a big bright loft in a renovated factory. Of course the week I had to pack and move was the hottest one of the summer, with temperatures and humidity in the nineties, and that old house had no air-conditioning and windows that stuck shut when they swelled. In those hot, airless rooms I packed up my married life — the carefully saved art my kids had made, my enormous stash of yarn, the Fiestaware and Italian pottery I'd collected. My final task: the rows and rows of books that lined three walls of one room.

Back when I moved into that house, on another summer day, I'd happily alphabetized the books, separating them into categories: fiction, memoir, biography, poetry, drama, reference. How happy I'd been that day as slowly the books took their places, as my daughter Grace twirled around the empty dining room (we couldn't yet afford a table and chairs for it) in her sparkly tutu and my son, Sam, sang "Wonder of Wonders" from *Fiddler on the Roof.* And what a contrast this moving day was, this taking down of all those books and putting them into boxes — FICTION A–C, FICTION M. Sam grown and living in Brooklyn, Grace dead fourteen years, my heart, once so full, now broken again.

I cried as I packed my books. And

I screamed. But I smiled too, a lot. As I held each book, deciding if I really needed to take it with me, I could remember reading — and sometimes rereading — it. Here were all my Alice Adams short story collections, a writer hardly known anymore but whose stories I still quote when I teach; my small paperback of Raymond Carver's *What We Talk About When We Talk About Love*, read on a New York City subway; *Bright Lights, Big City,* which I bought at the Spring Street Bookstore the day it came out; my dog-eared copies of *The Collected Stories of F. Scott Fitzgerald* and *So Long, See You Tomorrow;* three copies of C. S. Lewis's *A Grief Observed,* all given to me after Grace died to help soothe my grief, which it did (*"Her absence is like the sky,"* Lewis wrote, *"it covers everything"*). So many books, each of them returning a piece of myself to me — starry-eyed optimist, new writer, single Manhattan young woman, grief-stricken mother.

My new home had no built-in bookshelves, so my books stayed in the dozens and dozens of boxes until the new IKEA shelves were built; the older, smaller shelves found places in the loft; and still more bookshelves were bought and assembled. Until one day I looked up and the boxes were gone, the books — alphabetized and by genre — lined up again. *What is this life?* I ask myself almost every day as I look around at my new home, so big and open and sunny. I have two cats, Hermia and Gertrude, who sleep on my feet and lap. I've bought a turntable so that I can play my albums again, those songs of my youth also returned to me. And the lines that had so moved me as a teenager, that played even as I sat on my bed and read *Love Story*, move me still, perhaps even more true all these years later: *I have my books, and my poetry to protect me . . .*

Lesson 5: How to Write a Book

THE GRAPES OF WRATH

BY JOHN STEINBECK

If one book carried magic, imagine what four books could do. Four books nestled together in a box wrapped in red-and-green striped paper, topped with an extravagantly large bow, like a red dahlia had perched there, sitting under the Christmas tree with a tag bearing my name. Those four books were all by John Steinbeck, a writer most kids today have read by ninth grade when they were assigned *Of Mice and Men.* In my junior high, however, we weren't assigned novels. We read the short stories in our English literature textbook: "The Lottery" by Shirley Jackson; "Bartleby the Scrivener" by Herman Melville; "The Celebrated Jumping Frog of Calaveras County" by Mark Twain. And I loved those stories, loved taking essay tests on them and discussing them in class, loved reading them and thinking about them. Why did Bartleby *prefer not to*? What would I do if I was the one chosen in "The Lottery"? Could I have sat through Simon Wheeler's long story about Jim Smiley and his jumping frog?

But oh! A novel! And that Christmas of 1973, four novels!

"He's really good," my brother Skip said as I held that boxed set of Steinbeck in my hands. I wonder now if he saw that his gift made me cry? Somehow, he knew the real me; knew that I was someone who wanted nothing more than to read books; knew that, as C. S. Lewis said, "You can never get a book long enough to suit me." Two of those Steinbeck books were big, fat ones, the kind I loved to read most: *The Grapes of Wrath* and *East of Eden*. The other two were slender: *Of Mice and Men* and *Travels with Charley*.

Skip was telling me how Steinbeck had won both the Pulitzer Prize and the Nobel Prize for Literature. But I had no idea of the import of those prizes, or even what the distinction between them was. I managed to say thank you and to give him a quick kiss on his bearded cheek before I slipped away. Alone, with the twenty-four hours of Christmas music playing on the radio downstairs and the smell of Mama Rose's baking lasagna wafting up to me, I tore off the plastic and let the books drop from the box into my lap. I touched each cover in turn, held each book in my hand, opened to random pages. *"Charley is a mind-reading dog. There have been many trips in his lifetime . . ."* *"I remember about the rabbits, George . . ."* *"All great and precious things are lonely . . ."* And then this: *"To the red country and part of the gray of Oklahoma, the last rains came gently, and they did not cut the scarred earth.*"

I read that first line of *The Grapes of Wrath,* and I couldn't stop.

The Grapes of Wrath was published on April 14, 1939. Steinbeck wrote it in just four months, from June to October of 1938, when he was thirty-six years old. He put himself on a writing schedule to complete the novel in 100 days, averaging 2,000 words a day. Though some days, when the pressures of his life intruded (houseguests, buying and renovating a ranch) he only wrote 800 words, other days he wrote as many as 2,200. On October 26, he wrote the final 775 words and beneath them, in inch-and-a-half-high letters: "END."

Steinbeck had that ending in mind from the start, an image that he wrote toward, something the writer John Irving does too. "I have last chapters in my mind before I see first chapters," Irving told *The Paris Review* in 1986. "I usually begin with endings, with a sense of aftermath, of dust settling, of epilogue. I love plot, and how can you plot a novel if you don't know the ending first?"

When I finished reading *The Grapes of Wrath,* so many things about writing a novel became clear to me. Plot. Character. Conflict. Escalating stakes. Metaphor. *The Grapes of Wrath* begins with a drought and ends with a flood. Years later I would hear a lecture by a writer on this very device, which she called the rules of polarity. In my own novel *The Knitting Circle,* the protagonist, Mary, is empty-handed, both literally and emotionally, at the beginning; the final image is of abundance, Mary holding so much yarn that her arms are overflowing. When the Joads are in a rain-soaked barn at the end, I understood the impact of such a polarity.

In that barn they encounter a starving man and his son, whom the father had given their last bit of food. The dying man needs soup or milk to survive. The eldest Joad daughter, Rose of Sharon, has had a stillborn child. Ma Joad and Rose of Sharon *"looked deep into each other,"* and Rose of Sharon says, *"Yes."* Ma smiles: *"I knowed you would. I knowed."*

For a minute Rose of Sharon sat still in the whispering barn. Then she hoisted her tired body up and drew the comfort around her. She moved slowly to the corner and stood looking down at the wasted face, into the wide, frightened eyes. Then slowly she lay down beside him. He shook his head slowly from side to side. Rose of Sharon loosened one side of the blanket and bared her breast. "You got to," she said. She squirmed closer and pulled his head close. "There!" she said. "There." Her hand moved behind his head and supported it. Her fingers moved gently in his hair. She looked up and across the barn, and her lips came together and smiled mysteriously.

I had never read an ending that affected me like this one of Rose of Sharon giving her milk to the dying stranger. Speechless, I read the final scene again and again, its power never lessening. Even as a teenager, I understood the symbolism and power inherent in Rose of Sharon's selfless act. In *A Life in Letters,* Steinbeck said that he had "tried to make the reader participate in the actuality, what he [the reader] takes from it will be scaled entirely on his own depth or hollowness." Referring to there being five layers in the book, he added that "a reader will find as many as he can and he won't find more than he has in himself." It may seem hyperbolic, but I believe understanding this not only shaped me as a writer but also led me to become an English major when I went to college. I wanted more symbolism, more of those layers in literature. I wanted to find as many as I could, in both my reading and my writing life.

For years my math whiz brother was a mysterious blur in my life. Five years older than me, he mostly kept his distance from his bookworm little sister. I was, in the way of all little sisters, a nuisance. I cried if he sat too close to me in the backseat of the car. I cried when he got control of the television and forced me to sit through *Combat!* or *The Three Stooges.* I snooped on him and his first girlfriend, a tough-looking blonde with plum-colored suede boots and a leather miniskirt. I snooped on him and his buddies when they whispered together in his room, the air thick with exotic, musty, sweaty smells. He sat across from me at the dinner table, reigning over the bowl of mashed potatoes, getting extra pieces of steak from our grandmother, always the slide ruler nearby. "Does your face hurt?" he'd ask me. " 'Cause it's killing me!"

Then he was gone, off to college in his raspberry Bermuda shorts and matching polo shirt. I barely noticed. By then, I was entering junior high and my world became slumber parties and crushes on boys. I never even thought about Skip. Until he returned home that summer, now long-haired and wearing ripped jeans and pocket T-shirts, driving a lime-green V W Bug. He brought boys with him. And not just any boys, but *college* boys. Loads of them, each in their own V W Bug. Once again, he seemed to reign, this time over the picnic table in the backyard with a cooler of beer beside it. He worked that summer as a stock boy at Zayre, a local discount store, and there he acquired a cool, aloof, freckle-faced girlfriend who wore brown suede moccasins and a hard stare.

I kept a diary back then, mostly documenting how boring my life was. The one glimmer of emotion came in March of that year when I heard that Paul McCartney had gotten married. *Oh God,* I wrote, *please don't let it be true.* The next day's entry: *Bored.*

But when my brother's new girl-friend arrived, hanging back by the front door, glaring, clutching his hand, I began to write about her. And them. If I had been a more mature twelve-year-old, I might have recognized the sexual tension between them, understood that her constant desire to "go *now*" was sexual desire. Instead, they seemed oddly mysterious, with their whispering and disappearances. I became the Nancy Drew of romance, mistaking that sexual energy for what, I believed, must be love.

This, of course, made me even more of a nuisance. No, I couldn't go with them to the mall. Or for ice cream. Or on a walk. Or to the beach. Or anywhere. Still, I persisted in asking, and reported to my mother every time I was rebuked. My mother knew exactly what was going on, and she didn't like it, didn't like this brown-moccasined girl who kept my brother out late, made him miss dinner with the family, and wouldn't join a game of cards with us. *Take your sister,* she'd insist, and sometimes he would relent. I'd sit squeezed into the backseat of the Bug, watching his girlfriend's hand rub his thigh.

By Skip's junior year, they'd moved in together and he hardly came home at all that summer. And then, as his college graduation approached and he got a job with a chemical company in Connecticut, they announced they were getting married. Reluctantly, his fiancée asked me to be a bridesmaid, and she and her friends mostly ignored me through the endless bridal showers and gown fittings that ensued. The May day they got married I stood holding a bouquet of daisies, dressed in a pale yellow chiana gown, as "Sunrise, Sunset" played. But I was insignificant — to the wedding, and to my brother.

Or so I thought.

When he returned from his honeymoon in Europe later that summer, he brought me a gift — a cork box shaped like a windmill from Portugal. Perhaps he knew I was already chasing after windmills? We sat at the picnic table in the backyard together, his new gold wedding band glinting in the hot sun.

I asked him about his travels, and he told me that there was a shortage of cork trees and someday wine would all have twist-off caps. That was the thing about my brother, the thing I didn't realize until after he died nine years later. He was a visionary, always predicting technological advances and changes in the world as we knew it. Years later he would buy one of the first Betamaxes, showing me the miracle of taping television shows and watching them whenever you wanted to, zipping past the commercials. And a few years after that, he was one of the first people in the United States to get corrective eye surgery, restoring his bad eyesight to twenty-twenty vision and eliminating the need to wear glasses. So long ago was this that the surgery, performed by a Russian ophthalmologist, was done with scalpels instead of lasers.

That afternoon in our backyard, Skip asked me about myself, as if I were someone he'd just met. "What do you *do*?" he asked me. The answer was that I did a lot. I listed my activities: Marsha Jordan Girl, traveling back and forth to Boston to do fashion shows and mother-daughter teas, a floater at Jordan Marsh covering people's breaks and vacations in the Linens or Misses department. As I told him all this, he cocked his head and looked at me as if for the first time. He grinned. My brother had the most charming grin.

"Mostly," I said, "I read."

■ ■ ■ ■

Before skip gave me that boxed set
of Steinbeck, no one had ever given
me a book as a gift. But the gift was
even bigger than he'd imagined.
When I read the first line of *The
Grapes of Wrath* — *"To the red
country and part of the gray of Oklahoma, the last rains came gently,
and they did not cut the scarred
earth"* — some writerly thing broke
loose in me. "Spread a page with
shining," Steinbeck once advised
writers, and I could see that shine
as I read. I understood it. I had
read big, fat novels before, losing
myself in Victor Hugo's *Les Misérables* and Boris Pasternak's *Doctor Zhivago.* Those sweeping stories,

tragedies and triumphs spanning years and years, had captivated me for their otherness. But *The Grapes of Wrath* was so American, and the Joads so familiar somehow, and the language so lyrical, and the setting so real, that by reading it I saw what writers could do. And it dazzled me.

For years I had asked English teachers and guidance counselors how to become a writer. No one could tell me. John Steinbeck could though. *Write like this,* he seemed to be saying. *Tell our story. Tell your story.* Steinbeck intentionally wrote *The Grapes of Wrath* in five layers, intending to "rip the reader's nerves to rags by making him participate in its actuality." By writing

the novel this way, Steinbeck en-
sured it would have an impact on
all kinds of readers, and that impact
might be personal, historical, socio-
logical, or political. Grace Paley
said: "No story is ever one story,
it's always at least two. The one on
the surface and the one bubbling
beneath." I understood this somehow when I read *The Grapes of
Wrath,* those layers slowly revealing
themselves to me, showing me how
a novel can have such breadth and
touch anyone.

I only wish my brother had lived
to see my first novel in a bookstore
window. But he died on June 30,
1982, in his bathtub in Pittsburgh,
when he slipped and fell, drowning
in less than an inch of water. My

first novel, *Somewhere Off the Coast of Maine,* was published five years later. For years I had been writing a dreadful first novel called *The Betrayal of Sam Pepper,* about a woman in her mid-twenties living in Marblehead, Massachusetts, and feuding with a neighbor who has betrayed her boyfriend — in other words, a woman very much like me. How I toiled over that mess, staying up late at night to revise the pages I'd written in hotels on layovers as a TWA flight attendant. Some chapters sounded very much like imitation Hemingway, some like imitation Fitzgerald — which is exactly what they were. The plot meandered and grew preposterous, the dialogue was stilted, characters appeared and then vanished from the story, forgotten. Hundreds of handwritten pages.

The summer that my brother died, I moved home to be with my parents, until one day in August my mother told me to leave, to "go and live your life." What a gift that was, to free me from their grief. A few weeks later, I boarded an Amtrak train to New York City, my clothes and manuscript in a Hefty trash bag, $1,000 in my front jeans pocket. I moved into a tiny sublet on Sullivan Street in Greenwich Village, with a door topped with a piece of foam on a sawhorse for a bed. I had never lived alone and wasn't actually sure what to do. So I did what I always did — I wrote.

Except after what had happened to me that summer, *The Betrayal of Sam Pepper* seemed banal and facile and dull — which it was. I gathered all those hundreds of pages and threw them in the dumpster in front of my building. Then I sat down at my newly acquired electric typewriter and typed: *"To Sparrow her father was a man standing in front of a lime green VW van . . ."* The first line of my first published novel, *Somewhere Off the Coast of Maine.*

I began writing it the September after Skip died, trying, I see now, to understand what happened to him, to my family. I once heard an interview with the writer Kaye Gibbons in which she said all of her novels are about the death of her mother. Confused, the interviewer notes that none of her novels are about that. Gibbons said, "Oh, yes they are. Every one." Nowhere in that novel does a character resembling my brother appear, yet to me he is on every page.

Like many first novels, *Somewhere Off the Coast of Maine* tackled a lot of themes and topics: grief, friendship, love (romantic, parental, first love), cancer, the upheaval of the 1960s, the materialism of the 1980s, and even more. Overly ambitious perhaps, but I wanted those five layers that Steinbeck wrote about. All those years ago, on that Christmas when I sat on my yellow-and-white gingham bedspread and read *The Grapes of Wrath,* I understood viscerally and intellectually how good books illuminate so much more than the story on the surface, as Paley would say. True, the Joads are *"a people in flight,"* and the plot follows that flight from Oklahoma to California. But Steinbeck is also writing about the post-Depression urge for mobility and striving, political protests, the American Dream, desperate misery and suffering, disillusionment, and somehow hope. How I knew this as a sixteen-year-old reader, with no one with whom to share my ideas about literature, I cannot say. But I did know it, and I knew too that all I had to do to make my own dream of becoming a writer come true was to write every day, and to read every book I could get my hands on, to spread pages with shining.

Lesson 6: How to Fall in Love with Language

STANYAN STREET & OTHER SORROWS

BY ROD MCKUEN

"Onomatopoeia," my eighth-grade English teacher said. Then she wrote the strange word on the board. "A word that imitates the natural sound of the thing," she continued.

I copied the word into my notebook, my mind already excited by this new thing, this word with too many vowels.

"Whoosh," she was saying.

"Cock-a-doodle-doo. Splash. Bang."

Wait. There was a word for that? This was my first introduction to the world of literary devices, and I felt like a door had just opened into a kingdom where I belonged.

The teacher told us to write down examples of onomatopoeia, and once I began, I couldn't stop.

Rat-a-tat-tat. Plop. Slap. Rustle. Cuckoo.

I filled one lined page and began another. Buzz! Boom! Onomato-poeia!

That year, I was trying not to be the kid who always raised her hand with the right answer, the kid who kept asking questions long after the lesson had ended. My endless curi-osity for learning, my hunger to discuss everything with anyone, even sometimes exhausted my teachers. It definitely irritated my classmates. I had vowed to stop. But when the teacher asked for some examples of onomatopoeia, I couldn't control myself. I stood and read my forty-two examples, so thrilled by the sounds of those words and the fact that there was actually a name for them that when I'd read all the ones I'd written down, I kept talking because more examples of this lovely thing were still popping into my head.

"Snap, crackle, pop!" I said, delighted.

My classmates either glared at me or turned their glazed eyes toward the window, where autumn had just started to announce itself with a spattering of red and yellow leaves.

The teacher thanked me, then asked me to sit down, please.

The class clown said, "Belch," and everyone laughed. Except me. I was too busy to join in.

I grew up in a family that spoke Italian. In fact, most of the people in my neighborhood spoke Italian — black-clad women toting hand-made baskets full of eggplants and tomatoes they'd grown, musta-chioed men sitting at card tables on the sidewalk playing cards and smoking stogies. Our houses held two or three generations, our yards were gardens and orchards and chicken coops (no swing sets or tree houses), shrines to the Virgin Mary sat at the front door, and Italian filled the air. My great-grandmother spoke only Italian, no English. My grandmother spoke broken English. My mother and her siblings moved back and forth between the two languages, even when they were sitting around the kitchen table playing cards or gossiping. Usually they slipped into Italian when they didn't want us kids to understand what they were saying, perhaps about scoundrel uncles or loose women.

We were forbidden from learning Italian because these three generations had suffered so much cruelty and prejudice for being immigrants. They were made fun of for the lunches they brought to school, the smell of garlic and onions that emanated from their kitchens, their olive skin and large noses and larger families. They were called "wops" and "guineas"; they were told they were greasy and dirty. No, the older generations decided, we were going to be spared all that. We were going to be American. So Italian floated around me like a pleasant fog, a kind of poetry, I realize now. The older cousins mastered the swearwords, and taught those to us. They felt delicious on my tongue, those foreign dirty words, forbidden.

Auntie Angie used to sit with me when I was little and read the stories I'd written. There were seven girls and three boys in my mother's family, and Auntie Angie was the one who never had a daughter. Her son Stephen was the oldest of all the cousins, exactly ten years older than me, so that by the time I was in school he was off to college and then onto his life. Auntie Angie loved all her nieces, exotic birds in ruffled dresses.

One afternoon, when I was seven or eight, as I sat beside her at the enamel-topped kitchen table, she produced from the depths of her handbag a neatly folded newspaper clipping. She smoothed it out and told me to read it out loud.

" 'I never saw a Purple Cow,' " I read. " 'I never hope to see one. But I can tell you, anyhow, I'd rather see than be one!' "

Auntie Angie hooted with laughter. "This guy, Ogden Nash, he makes the best rhymes!"

Why this poem was in the newspaper, or how Auntie Angie had heard of Ogden Nash, I cannot say. What I do know is that reading that nonsense poem out loud, feeling the rhymes slide off my tongue, reaching the delightful ending — *I'd rather see than be one!* — was an experience that I still can't describe, like the first time you ride your bike without training wheels or watch television in color instead of black and white. A world opened up.

Perhaps seeing my surprised expression, Auntie Angie said, "It's a *poem.* It *rhymes.*"

Poem. Rhyme. Still a wonderful mystery even as I read it over and over, with Auntie Angie explaining that "cow" and "anyhow" rhyme.

Finally she went back into that bottomless handbag and retrieved a small lined notebook and Bic pen. "Here," she said, "you write down some rhymes."

I stared at the blank paper until Auntie Angie, muttering, "Jesus, let me start," made columns with words at the top: "Hair." "Car." "Dog." Not unlike the day years later when I understood onomato-poeia, I began to write, slowly at first and then with wild abandon. Words tumbled from my brain. I was rhyming!

Auntie Angie lit a fresh Pall Mall and checked my list from time to time, but mostly went back to talking with her sisters. Before she left, she turned to a fresh page in the notebook and said, "When I come back, find a rhyme for this word." And in perfect block letters, she wrote: PURPLE.

For several agonizing days, I struggled unsuccessfully to find a word that rhymed with "purple." Maybe she would forget, I hoped. Maybe she wouldn't come back. Neither of these possibilities were even remotely likely to happen. Auntie Angie never forgot anything. And, like all of my aunts and uncles, she came to visit three or four or even five times a week. Sure enough, one afternoon I came home from school and there she was, Pall Mall dangling between her red-lipsticked lips.

"Well?" she asked almost immediately.

I swallowed hard and reluctantly admitted, "No word rhymes with purple."

"Ha! That's not what our friend Ogden Nash says!"

Years later I would learn that Ogden Nash hadn't invented that nonsense rhyme. But at that moment, I hated him. And maybe even Auntie Angie.

"Maple surple rhymes with purple!" Auntie Angie said, and laughed good and hard.

I frowned. Maple surple wasn't a

thing or a word. But slowly I understood. Words and rhymes were fun. You could play with them, mix them up, turn them around, rearrange letters, make things up. Grinning, I climbed onto Auntie Angie's lap. She dug into that giant handbag again, pulled out the notebook and pen, and told me to do some rhyming. Yes, I was back in love with Auntie Angie, but I was in love with something else too, something big and strange and thrilling: language.

First there was onomatopoeia, and then there was simile — *as blue as the sky, as blue as denim, blue like the morning,* I wrote — and then metaphor and haiku and sonnets.

Suddenly my world of prose was broken up and all I wanted to do was write poetry. We read "Annabel Lee" and "The Raven" and "Richard Cory" and "The Road Not Taken." We got extra credit for memorizing Oliver Goldsmith's "The Deserted Village." How I loved sitting alone in my room, saying that poem aloud: *Sweet Auburn, loveliest village of the plain, / Where health and plenty cheered the laboring swain . . .*

It did not occur to me that somewhere in the library sat volumes of poetry. It seemed to me a precious thing, a poem, and I could not begin to imagine where poems resided. But one night as I played my favorite album, Simon and Garfunkel's *Sounds of Silence,* it struck me that its eponymous song was actually a poem. Wasn't *darkness, my old friend* personification? And *words like silent raindrops fell* a simile? *The neon God* a metaphor? I played the song over and over, a notebook in hand, teasing out its meaning. Then I turned my attention to *I am a rock* — metaphor! *I am an island!* When we had to write a paper on our favorite poet, my classmate Nancy wrote hers on Robert Frost and Steven wrote his on Edgar Allan Poe. But me, I wrote mine on Paul Simon.

One Saturday when I was in tenth grade, as I made my circuit around the Warwick Mall, a book caught

my eye in the window at Waldenbooks. Slim, with an electric-blue
cover and yellow and white letters
that reminded me of a Peter Max
poster, it read *Stanyan Street &*
Other Sorrows in yellow, and above
it, in white, the name Rod Mc-
Kuen. Beside it was another Rod
McKuen book, *Lonesome Cities.*
Also slim, with a moody gray cover
of clouds and, in the same psyche-
delic type-face, the title in hot pink.
I went inside the bookstore, and
picked up *Stanyan Street & Other*
Sorrows.

"The words within these pages
are for music," the inside flap read.
"They sing of love lost and found
and lost again. They are hymns to
the dying, sonnets to the summer

and verses of the joy of being wanted — even for a night." All of the poems were written by Rod McKuen, the flap said, one of the finest chansonniers in the country. Later, of course, back at home, I went directly to my Reader's Digest dictionary and looked up the word "chansonnier": a poet-songwriter, solitary singer, who sang his or her own songs. But standing there with that book in my hand, it only mattered that I was holding a book of poetry, a book that spoke of dying and summer and loneliness, the very things that I paced my room worrying about at night.

The poems themselves were slight, most just two or three short stanzas. But they were so profound,

I thought. They weren't like the few we'd read in school, which though I'd loved their rhythm and rhyme were formal and complicated. These poems by Rod McKuen seemed to speak directly to me, perhaps directly to every teenager in 1970. *"Sometimes I think people were meant to be strangers . . ."* Why at the tender age of fourteen I felt so lonely and alienated I cannot say. But when Paul Simon sang, *"I am a rock, I am an island,"* my heart screamed, "I am too!" And when Rod McKuen wrote about not getting close to others to avoid damaging your heart, it sounded like he had read what was in *my* heart.

I knew nothing of love, having

only kissed a boy once at the Rocky Point amusement park the summer before. But I believed what Rod McKuen wrote: *"I know that love is worth all the time it takes to find."* *"Think of that,"* he said, *"when all the world seems made of . . . empty pockets."* I too would be *"content to live on the sound your stomach makes,"* content to eat *"marmalade and oysters for breakfast."* *"If you keep the empty heart alive a little longer / love will come. / It always does . . ."* he wrote in "Some Thoughts for Benson Green on His 27th Birthday." Yes! I thought as I read. I could keep my empty heart alive!

In "Spring Song" he asked: *"Where were you when I was grow-*

ing up and needed somebody?" Standing in that Waldenbooks, I began to weep when I read that line. As much as I'd loved to carefully write the rhyme patterns on poems at school and to ponder their meanings, Rod McKuen's free-form poems made me feel like he was whispering secrets to me. I memorized the simile that ended "State Beach" — *"the rain comes down like tears"* — and wrote it in my purple lined notebook with all the other snippets of songs and sentences I collected there.

I don't remember how much the book cost, surely no more than six or seven dollars, but whatever it cost was too expensive for me. Instead, every Saturday when I

went to the mall, I stood memoriz-
ing the poems in *Stanyan Street &
Other Sorrows,* and later in *Listen
to the Warm* and *Lonesome Cities.*
Even now, long after I've learned
better poems, long after I've fallen
in love with E. E. Cummings and
Emily Dickinson and Elizabeth
Bishop, I can still recite Rod Mc-
Kuen's poem "Ellen's Eyes": *"All
the space is taken up / remembering
Ellen's eyes."*

From the distance of so many de-
cades, I understand the appeal to a
yearning, dreamy young girl of a
chansonnier who wrote about the
beach and the rain, both of which
remain important to me. I even
understand how all that loneliness

spoke to me, a girl who felt alone in the world in which she lived. But I see too how those poems reflected my yearning to leave my familiar world. And in 1970, when teen-agers left home, they went to San Francisco. The Summer of Love had been just the year before, and magazines and newspapers printed photographs of hippies every day, long-haired girls with flowers in their hair and blue-jeaned barefoot boys in Haight-Ashbury. Even a group as seemingly benign as the Cowsills sang about loving the flower girl, who sits smiling in the rain with flowers in her hair — *Flowers everywhere!*

Part of what seduced me on that long-ago Saturday afternoon at the

Warwick Mall was the poetry of Kearny Street and Sausalito, of hills and fog, of San Francisco. Years later, when I went to San Francisco for the first time, I got a map from the hotel concierge and had him point out Stanyan Street to me. Then I made my way there, to Haight-Ashbury and that street lined with Victorian houses. All of the girls who wore flowers in their hair were long gone by then, and Stanyan Street looked very different from what I'd imagined. Yet when I looked up at the street sign with its name on it, I remembered the poem of that name: *"I have total recall of you / and Stanyan Street / because I know it will be important later . . ."*

How could I know all those years ago how important these words and Paul Simon's and Ogden Nash's and that afternoon when the world broke open and I learned about onomatopoeia would be? How all of these things, these poems, turned me into a lover of language and its infinite joys. Pop! Boom! In that moment on Stanyan Street, I saw that girl standing in that bookstore in that mall, clutching a slim neon-blue volume of poems that promised someday she would fall in love, be loved, and find herself in San Francisco. Even that young girl knew that such is the power of poetry, a gift that stayed with her the rest of her life.

Lesson 7: How to Be Curious

A STONE FOR DANNY FISHER

BY HAROLD ROBBINS

As a teenager I read indiscriminately. At the library, as I've said, I
usually chose books by their size —
the fatter the better. Although that
meant that I discovered Victor
Hugo and Tolstoy and Dickens by
the time I was fifteen, it also meant
that I read — and, I admit, loved
— Irving Wallace, Jacqueline Su-
sann, and Harold Robbins with
equal fervor. In one week I might
read *Anna Karenina* and *Hawaii,* the
next *Les Misérables* and *Valley of*

the Dolls. I devoured Evan Hunter's *Paper Lions* with as much intensity as I did *Great Expectations.* Doris Lessing could have been talking about me and my reading habits when she said, "With a library you are free . . . it is the most democratic of institutions because no one — but no one at all — can tell you what to read and when and how."

When I look back on the books that shaped me, the ones that taught me how to think and live and dream, a surprising one keeps coming into my mind: *A Stone for Danny Fisher* by Harold Robbins. The cover screams bodice ripper. A raven-haired beauty half reclines on a bed, wearing a silky black slip and stockings held up by garters. Below, a glistening shirtless Danny Fisher stares down at a man he has just knocked out in a boxing ring. When I began to reread it again a half century later I could hear the advice I give writing students: don't overuse the action of looking; don't repeat words; don't use ellipses; stay in the point of view; avoid sentimentality and melodrama — all of which Robbins employs on every page. The plot revolves around Danny, a young Jewish boy who at eight years old moves with his family to a home he loves in Brooklyn. He acquires a dog and friends in short order and soon even learns that the older teenage girl across the street likes to leave her shades up so he can watch her undress, something that makes him feel filthy. Danny punishes himself by taking showers so cold they hurt.

There's lots of sex in *A Stone for Danny Fisher,* though often I couldn't tell if he had just kissed someone, actually had sex with her, or just felt her breasts. More than once I had to reread scenes, confused by Danny's feelings of guilt after being with a girl. But second and even third reads left me just as confused. Perhaps these vague sex scenes were just right for my naïve teenage self — enough to titillate but not enough to terrify me.

One night, Danny's parents and sister go to the movies, leaving him home alone. Mimi, the girl who sexually taunts him from across the street, comes to his house and tries to seduce him in one of the strangest seduction scenes I've ever read. Of course, as a fifteen-year-old, confused by sex myself, it must have seemed sexually charged and exciting to read. Mimi holds a tumbler of cold water, then puts her cold hands on Danny's face. He doesn't move or respond. So she presses her lips against his and bends him backward across the sink, at which point Danny grabs her by the shoulders and squeezes so hard that she gasps in pain, which makes him laugh. *"Don't fight with me, Danny,"* Mimi tells him. *"I like you. And I can tell you like me!"* They hear a car in the driveway and Mimi leaves. So why is Danny racked with guilt? What did they even do that made him feel *"soiled and dirty"*? Not only does Danny take one of those frigid showers, he also slaps himself so hard that he doubles over in pain. Often these scenes are followed by such cruelty toward the girl that Danny seems almost insane. When Danny sees Mimi again the next day, he stares at her coldly and then tells her, *"I hate your guts."*

Surely, I thought after I read this scene as an adult, I had read this book over and over as pure escapism. Although I didn't have very discerning taste as a fifteen-year-old, I could see this book for what it was. Even now I like to sometimes indulge in the guilty pleasure of reading a book that literary snobs would never consider reading. And I enjoy them, those paperbacks I don't mind leaving behind on an airplane. They make long flights pass pleasantly. I don't have to marvel at the use of language or metaphor or puzzle over how the author pulled off such a mind-bogglingly intricate plot. I just read it and forget it, perhaps a habit I learned back in high school when I read any book I could get my hands on.

But then why did *A Stone for Danny Fisher* come to mind immediately when thinking of books that shaped me, right beside *The Grapes of Wrath* and *Rabbit, Run*? I cannot say with honesty that when I read it back in 1971 or '72 that I recognized it as a lesser literary achievement. In fact, I remember loving it, every word. I remember how hard I sobbed when Danny's dog dies, and when he visits the Brooklyn home his family was forced to leave, when he dies at the end, and at the book's final line: *"To live in the hearts we leave behind is not to die."* I also remember that after reading it several times, I took out other Harold Robbins books and couldn't even finish them. I didn't like them at all. No, *this* novel spoke to me.

As I reread *A Stone for Danny Fisher* this past summer, slowly I understood. I believe that magically the book we are supposed to read somehow appears in our hands at just the right time. This happened for me when I struggled to manage multiple points of view as I wrote my first novel, *Somewhere Off the Coast of Maine.* Perhaps out of fear of writing an entire novel, I'd considered the book as interconnected short stories. But here I was, trying to make those stories a novel. Pages covered my living room floor in my Bleecker Street apartment. What was I thinking, trying to use so many points of view? Convinced I would never figure out how to make it work, and that I would have to give back my advance, I decided to take a long walk. I ended up at the Spring Street Bookstore in Soho, where I picked up a book by a writer I'd never heard of before — Anne Tyler. The book was *Dinner at the Homesick Restaurant,* and it was written in multiple points of view, a detail I didn't know when I bought it. Back at my apartment, I ignored all the pages on my floor and flopped, dejected, onto the couch. I read that novel straight through — enchanted, yes, but also, I know now, learning from it how to manage the narrative style. Recently I read that Tyler had originally written *Dinner at the Homesick Restaurant* as interconnected stories too. That book landed in my hands at just the right time. And now I realize so did *A Stone for Danny Fisher.*

■ ■ ■ ■

In the summer of 1970, my brother, Skip, brought home a new girlfriend. His high-school girlfriend, Weezie, had been a freckle-faced, big-toothed girl whom I loved. She treated me like a kid sister and happily gave me extra scoops of ice cream when I went to the Newport Creamery at the mall, where she worked. But Weezie broke Skip's heart, and the summer after his freshman year at college, at his job at Zayre, he met the girl he would eventually marry, the one who appeared in our kitchen one hot, muggy night, wearing torn jeans and moccasins, a type of shoe my mother believed only "bad girls" wore. Where she got such an idea I don't know, but she also believed — and still does — that "bad girls" drink soda straight out of a bottle instead of using a straw. To this day I have never seen my mother lift a bottle of soda to her lips. She sips from a straw.

The moccasins were the least of the problem, however. The girl was Jewish, which did not bother my parents (though my Italian grandmother didn't much like it), but infuriated *her* parents. So much so that they forbade Skip from dating their daughter or even calling her. *That* infuriated my mother, who didn't like anybody who did anything against her kids. Barring Skip from their house was an insult to her, to all of us, and so a kind of war between the two families began. When the girl's father called my father and insisted my parents keep Skip away from his daughter, my mother took the phone and gave him a piece of her mind. Who the hell did he think he was anyway? I listened, afraid and excited in equal measure. Somehow we were in a feud — the Hatfields and McCoys, the Capulets and Montagues. It all seemed terribly romantic to me.

Although my family was Catholic, we were not really churchgoers. My father, who had converted from Baptist to Catholic back in 1950 in order to marry my mother, liked the folk masses at Sacred Heart

Church and happily went once or twice a month to sing "Day by Day" and "Michael, Row Your Boat Ashore" while the young priest strummed the guitar. When he first met my mother, her family didn't like him — he was a sailor, he wasn't Catholic, and worst of all, he wasn't Italian. His Midwestern family viewed my mother as some kind of exotic creature because she was Italian and Catholic. Their nicknames for her — unbelievable now — were "wop" and "fish eater," the latter because Catholics didn't eat meat on Fridays. When she offered to make them spaghetti and meatballs during a visit to Indiana, she was shocked that she couldn't find some of the ingredients — parmesan cheese, fresh parsley, garlic. Still, even without these key things, they marveled at the meal. They'd never tasted anything like it.

But all of that was twenty years earlier, and in time my grandmother fell in love with my father. The two of them fried the crispelles and baked the sweet bread at Easter, and cleaned the eel and calamari for the Feast of the Seven Fishes on Christmas Eve. Religious differences seemed old-fashioned and trivial by 1970. We knew exactly one Jewish person: Jean Goldstein, a friend of my auntie Emma. She arrived at our house a few times a year, always heavily tanned and shiny with gold and diamond jewelry. Jean Goldstein became an emblem of our family's openness in this war. "Jean Goldstein sits right at this table and eats sausage and peppers!" my mother would remind us after another call from Phil, the girl's angry father. "I would never tell Jean Goldstein she wasn't welcome in my house. Who does he think he is?"

My family had no understanding of the Jewish religion or of Jewish history. Mama Rose believed the Jews had killed Jesus, so she didn't trust them. Surely my parents knew about the Holocaust, but to what degree I cannot say. And as terrible as it sounds, religion just didn't matter to them and therefore they couldn't accept it as such a big deal

— big enough to cause all this trouble. That summer, and into the fall and winter, we got calls that the girl had run off to be with my brother at college; calls insisting that we had to do something, make Skip leave her alone. The calls often came late at night, and I would hear my father's weary voice say, "The more you try to stop them, the more they'll want to be together. If you let them see each other, this thing will blow over."

It didn't. Instead, at the tender age of twenty, my brother announced they were getting married. My parents had married at nineteen and twenty-one, so they weren't bothered that Skip was so young. But he also announced that he was converting to Judaism, which did not go over very well. Mama Rose cried, claiming he was breaking Jesus's heart and that he wouldn't be able to get into heaven. "What about Christmas?" my mother said, and she was crying too. Even though we were only nominally Catholic in many ways, my mother held on to certain aspects of the faith. She considered saying something against Catholicism blasphemous. "Jesus cries," she'd tell us if we questioned a tenet or told a joke that involved a priest. She says her prayers — Hail Mary, the Lord's Prayer, and the Act of Contrition — every night. She loves the Virgin Mary and all the saints, especially Saint Anthony.

How would having a Jewish son fit into this construct of her faith? My father, on the other hand, didn't really care. "It's just words," he said. "What matters is who you are, not what you are."

With the announcement of the conversion, the girl's parents were suddenly our best friends. Phil brought my father cigars and Eileen went shopping for mother-of-the-bride and mother-of-the-groom dresses with my mother. They came over for Christmas Eve, happily eating shrimp cocktail and drinking my father's special punch: Hawaiian Punch, rum, strawberries, and rainbow sherbet. As the wedding neared, we saw them more than we saw almost anyone else.

There were decisions to be made on color schemes and tablecloths and yarmulkes. My isolated world of Catholic immigrants was all at once steeped in Judaism. And at the same time, in that magical way books have, I slid *A Stone for Danny Fisher* off the library shelf. Attracted by its size — 494 pages! — and perhaps by that sexy cover, I inadvertently picked a book at least nominally about Judaism.

Just about everyone in my hometown was Catholic. In second grade the class showed up on the playground one spring morning with our foreheads smudged with ashes. This happened every Ash Wednesday. Before school we went to church and got our ashes. But that year I noticed one girl with a clean, shiny forehead. Her name was Sandra Goldsmith, and I approached her that morning with a great deal of curiosity. Maybe she was going to get her ashes after school, I thought. Ash Wednesday marked the first day of Lent, and the talk on the playground that morning was about what everyone was giving up for Lent — candy, soda, television.

"What are you giving up for Lent?" I asked Sandra.

She kicked at the pavement with the toe of her scuffed brown shoe and shrugged.

"I'm giving up candy," I offered, already missing the flying saucers filled with tiny beads of sugary candy that I preferred.

Sandra remained silent.

I still remember the moment so clearly, remember the bewilderment I felt at her behavior. Even though I went to a public school, playground conversation often involved discussions about Pope Paul VI and when the secrets of Fátima would be revealed. We were kids or grandkids of immigrants, French Canadians and Italians and Portuguese and Polish Catholics who had come to work in the textile mills that still lined the river that cut through town. That there were people in the world who were not Catholic never occurred to me.

"When are you getting your

ashes?" I asked, not meaning to bully.

Sandra finally looked up, her cheeks red and wet with tears. "I'm not Catholic!" she blurted.

Before I could ask her what that meant — what were you if not Catholic? — Sandra ran out of the playground gate, down the sidewalk toward home.

Ten years later, I had a Jewish brother.

During skip's conversion I learned about the Jewish High Holy Days, the stories of Passover and Chanukah; I learned what it meant to keep kosher and what a family did on the Sabbath; I learned that some Jews wouldn't use elevators or turn off lights from sunset Friday to sunset Saturday. To me, it sounded mysterious and exotic. Then I read *A Stone for Danny Fisher* and, coincidentally, was cast as Tzeitel in my high school's production of *Fiddler on the Roof.*

I had learned how to live through reading a lot of books, with a smattering of pop culture thrown in. And that year I learned about the pogroms in Russia, why Jews covered their heads and wore prayer shawls, and the importance of keeping their faith — all through a Broadway musical. With kerchiefs on our heads and aprons over our dresses, we sang "Matchmaker, Matchmaker," and we danced with brooms and clasped our hands together as we twirled to "Tradition." During my marriage to the tailor Motel Kamzoil, the cast picked me up as I sat on a chair and danced, holding me aloft. Two months later I watched this happen at my brother's wedding, shortly after he and his bride took their vows to "Sunrise, Sunset."

A Stone for Danny Fisher opens at Mount Zion Cemetery a week before the High Holy Days. *"For this is the week that Lord God Jehovah calls His angels about Him and opens before them the Book of Life. And your name is inscribed on one of those pages. Written on that page will be your fate for the coming days,"* it begins, and then continues to explain that the book remains open for six days, during which you devote yourself to acts of charity, such as visiting the dead. To make sure you get credit for your visit, *"you will pick up a small stone from the earth beneath your feet and place it on the monument so the Recording Angel will see it when he comes through the cemetery each night."*

Although much of the novel deviates from an exploration of Judaism, Danny's Jewishness is established from the start. In the first chapter, two boys corner Danny in his new neighborhood and demand to know which church he will attend. When he tells them, *"I'm a Jew and I go to shul,"* one of the boys snarls, *"Why did you kill*

Christos?" Reading this, surely I remembered my own interrogation of Sandra Goldsmith on the playground and my grandmother telling Skip that the Jews killed Christ. In the next chapter, Danny has his bar mitzvah, the scene rich with details of the synagogue and the ceremony. After school I was watching the boys in the cast of *Fiddler* practice singing "To Life" and in my bed at night I was reading about Danny's parents shouting it to him at his bar mitzvah. Robbins describes the white silk tallith emblazoned with a blue Star of David and the white silk yarmulke that Danny wears; a few months later I sat in a synagogue at my brother's wedding looking out at a sea of men wearing yellow yarmulkes to match the couple's color theme.

I don't remember the confluence of these events — my brother's conversion and marriage, reading *A Stone for Danny Fisher,* and performing in *Fiddler on the Roof* — striking me then as important. But from the distance of years I see how a bestselling book and a popular musical helped me navigate the changes in my family, how they showed me through songs and stories a glimpse into a world I had been, until then, unaware of.

In all the years that have followed, I have visited dozens of countries and witnessed countless traditions and cultures. I've attended a voodoo ceremony in Brazil and visited a witch doctor in Uganda. I've been splattered with paint during the festival of Holi in India and heard the muezzin call Muslims to prayer in Egypt; I've seen single women wear their hair in braids by law in Turkmenistan and pilgrims approach temples on their knees in Tibet. All of these things, and so many more, I've watched with curiosity and an open heart. Thanks in no small part to Harold Robbins, Joseph Stein, Jerry Bock, and Sheldon Harnick, who showed me a glimpse of a world and a belief different from my own.

LESSON 8: HOW TO HAVE SEX

THE HARRAD EXPERIMENT

BY ROBERT H. RIMMER

I had exactly two lessons in sex education. The first came from my ninth-grade, gray-haired, bespectacled home economics teacher. Mrs. Follett taught the cooking half of home ec, but one day she led all of us girls (the boys were busy building bookends in shop class in the basement) to the gym and showed us an antiquated-looking film on menstruation. We sat on the bleachers, horrified at the dancing cartoon ovaries and fallopian tubes and giggling as the bobby-soxed girls asked an offscreen interviewer why they suffered with pimples, cramps, and moodiness.

After the movie, Mrs. Follett brought us back into the home ec room with its stoves and mixing bowls and deep sinks, stood in front of us wearing a serious expression, and said, "Girls, there's a difference between necking and petting. Necking is above the pearls, and petting is below the pearls. Necking is okay. Petting is not."

She nodded solemnly, then handed out recipe cards for fudgies.

I'm sure I wasn't the only one in this classroom full of daughters of immigrants — Italian and Portuguese and Irish, our mothers at work in mills or diners or industrial cafeterias — who felt confused. Pearls? Who in this town wore pearls? And what was *above* them? I thought of pictures I'd seen of flappers with their long strands of pearls skimming the hems of their short dresses. I thought of the movies I watched on television on Sunday afternoons with Doris Day or Grace Kelly in cocktail dresses, a necklace of pearls at their collarbones. Where, then, was the line between necking and petting? I needed specifics, clarity, my own set of pearls that fell to the perfect safe length.

Marie Mattias, my cooking partner, had already donned her apron and was collecting the ingredients for our fudgies. It was rumored that she had already kissed a boy, so perhaps this necking/petting thing made sense to her. I watched her place sugar and milk, butter and cocoa powder, rolled oats and peanut butter on our workstation. Beside us, my friend Jane was frowning — not at the recipe but at everything that had happened that afternoon, the dancing ovaries, the discussion of pimples, the pearls.

I lined a baking sheet with wax paper and joined Marie in dumping all the ingredients into a saucepan. We didn't have to bake the cookies, just drop them by the tablespoonful onto the wax paper and put them in the refrigerator for thirty minutes. When they had cooled and hardened, we would place them onto a silver serving tray and bring them to the boys in shop class. It smelled good down there, musty and woodsy at the same time. When we walked in, the boys lifted their goggles onto their heads and devoured our cookies while we watched.

Later — not that day or even the next, but weeks later — I went home after school with Marie. We were on double sessions: the seventh and eighth graders went to school from seven to noon; we ninth graders went from twelve thirty to five thirty. Marie lived up the street from the school, in one half of a mill house. It was almost dark by the time school ended, and the autumn air smelled of leaves burning and the sharp scent of winter approaching. At her house, her brother lazed on the sofa. He wore blue jeans and a pocket T-shirt, and although he was barefoot he had drawn what looked like the straps of sandals across the arches of his feet, ending in a pointed V between his big toe and the one beside it. This, Marie explained, allowed him to enter restaurants and stores barefoot, as clerks and waitresses thought he had on sandals. The Mattiases had a dog named Frog, and Marie and her brother liked to give him a tablespoon of peanut butter and then watch him try to swallow it. We made fudgies, and while we waited for them to cool we gave Frog peanut butter and watched him smack it loudly on his tongue.

When the cookies were ready, Marie pulled out a Ouija board.

"Ask it anything," she said.

I looked at her curly hair and black-lined eyes.

"What's a French kiss?" I asked.

We placed our hands on the planchette and waited. Slowly, haltingly, it moved across the board, spelling out: KISSING WITH TONGUE. Grossed out, I lifted my hands suddenly from the planchette, just as Marie nudged it toward *S*. Our eyes met briefly. I stood and said I had to go home.

Kissing with tongues?

My second sex education lesson came, in a way, from my mother. As a Catholic, I was told that a girl saved herself for marriage long before I understood what exactly I was saving. "You don't buy the cow if the milk is free," my mother would tell me, another thing I did not understand. What were girls giving away? And why, if boys wanted it, did they not want the girl? If I prodded my mother for answers, she did not respond. The last thing my prudish mother wanted to do was talk about sex. "Let me just say," she told me once, eyes averted, cheeks red, "you have to *really* love a man to do that with him." What was *that*? I wondered. And why was it so mysterious, so valuable, yet so disgusting?

My mother and my aunts had a terrible term for promiscuous women, one that disturbed me then and disturbs me even more so now. "She's a pig," they'd say about the divorcée who dated lots of men or the teenager who got pregnant. Today, I ask my mother not to use that word to describe any woman. But as a girl I just cringed. One thing I knew for certain was that I never wanted to be called that. I had no concept of how girls got pregnant, or even of how sex worked. Once I heard Joan Rivers on *The Merv Griffin Show* say that she'd read *The Joy of Sex* and took its advice by wrapping her naked body in Saran Wrap and greeting her husband, Edgar, at the door like that. The audience laughed but I only felt confused. The next time I went to Waldenbooks at the mall, I found *The Joy of Sex* and flipped through it. The illustrations of naked men and women, pubic hair drawn in squiggly lines, arms and legs thrust in every direction, looked disgusting. "You *really* have to love a man to do that."

I was twelve when I got my first period, an event I only anticipated or knew about because my cousin, a year older, got hers the year before. For months I hoped I'd find blood on my underwear, but when nothing happened I forgot about it.

Then I went to a birthday party for a girl with the magical name of Staria (at some point it lost its magic when I learned her mother had plucked it from a book about a horse with that name). Staria lived in a new development and had many wonderfully exotic things to marvel at — her family ate at a kitchen table that had benches instead of chairs, for one thing. And her basement was not dirt-floored like mine, or a second kitchen like the ones so many people I knew had, but rather was bright and large with indoor/outdoor carpeting and a door that led outside into the yard. At the party there was a long table with all kinds of mayonnaise-y food —

tuna salad and egg salad — something I'd never seen before. We didn't even have a jar of mayonnaise at home.

"It's time for lunch," Staria's mother announced.

I wore a hot-pink minidress with a scalloped hem and white go-go boots, an outfit bought just for the occasion. As soon as her mother told us it was time for lunch, I stood and went to the buffet table (though of course I didn't know that's what it was called, having never heard the word "buffet" before), peering at those finger sandwiches, taking the least offensive-looking one and piling chips onto my plate. There was a hot tray of tiny meatballs in red currant jelly. I took two on their cellophane-tipped toothpicks just to be polite. Where I came from, meatballs were large and covered in red sauce. When I looked up, I saw that I was the first one getting food. Everyone else had formed a line and was waiting. Everyone except a soft-spoken girl named Nancy, who still sat primly perched at the edge of her chair.

"Ann," Staria said, "since you went first, you can't be Miss Peanut."

Miss Peanut? Clearly I had done something wrong, but I had no idea what it was. Hadn't Staria's mother told us it was time to eat? My stomach cramped. The smell of mayonnaise, unfamiliar and sweet (perhaps it was actually Miracle Whip?), wafted upward and I had to swallow a wave of nausea.

"Miss Peanut is polite," Staria continued, "and lets others go first."

Now my stomach was really hurting, and something strange began — I had my first headache, a pounding that was thunderous and painful. I thought I might have to go to the bathroom — there was one down there! In the basement! Staria's mother had pointed it out to us when we arrived.

"Today," Staria announced, "Miss Peanut is Nancy!"

Nancy blushed a deep red. Staria grinned at her, and as she went to bring Nancy a large prize of some kind, my stomachache got so bad that I ran to the bathroom. I'm sure that the other kids thought I'd left out of embarrassment for being the antithesis of Miss Peanut. Crammed into the tiny bathroom — her mother had called it a "half-bath" — I yanked down my under-wear and there it was: two smears of dark red blood.

That afternoon, after I snuck upstairs and called my mother on Staria's fake old-fashioned crank telephone that hung on the kitchen wall, trying not to cry; after my mother picked me up and I left the party without saying goodbye or thank you; after my mother silently handed me a strange belt and a box of sanitary napkins; after she showed me how to attach the napkins to the belt; she handed me a slender, mustard-colored paperback, almost more of a pamphlet, with a silhouette of a young woman's face and some vague title about mothers and daughters. "Read this," she told me, and I dutifully did, a hot water bottle on my aching stomach, a bulge of Kotex between my legs. The book told me this would happen every twenty-eight days, that I could get pregnant on day fourteen of my cycle, that boys had a penis that resembled a mushroom and a sack below it that contained two balls the size of plums.

Was it any surprise, then, that when someone showed up in ninth grade with a book called *The Harrad Experiment,* a novel about fictional Harrad College and its experiment to have men and women live together and feel free to have sex, argue about politics and philosophy, change partners, and think and act "freely," I eagerly read it? And reread it, especially the dog-eared pages 160–167, which describe the act of sex and orgasms in graphic detail? So, I thought, this is what all the fuss is about.

The Harrad Experiment was published in hardcover in 1966, and in paperback a year later. The copy that was surreptitiously passed around my ninth-grade classroom was that original paperback, with a naked college-age boy draping a sheet around a naked girl's shoulders. They are both tanned and blond, he looking down at her, she looking directly at the reader. It was racy and titillating, that cover. Reading the book as I did in 1970, when teenagers were moving in droves to Haight-Ashbury in search of free love and just a few years earlier *Time* magazine had featured the Pill on its cover, it seemed to me to be a poster for just that. Initially, Sherbourne Press printed 10,000 mail-order copies sold through an ad in *Playboy* magazine because the novel was too racy for bookstores. But Bantam promoted the paperback edition that I read with sexy billboards and advertisements. It sold 300,000 copies within a month. Eventually, more than 3 million copies were sold, with reviews posted on Amazon as recently as February 2016.

One of the rules at Harrad College is that all sports, exercise, and swimming in the pool had to be done in the nude, an idea that I found impossible to imagine. That year, in ninth grade, we had to change out of our clothes and into our gym uniform in tiny shared dressing rooms connected to smelly, moldy showers. My dressing room partner was a girl named Joanne, who, out of embarrassment or perhaps out of bravery, would hustle into our small space, whip off her clothes, and pull on the one-piece pale blue gym uniform, seemingly in one motion. I caught a flash of her flesh, pink and still baby chubby, and then she was snapping up the front snaps while I tried to strategically drape my towel in a way that would hide as much as possible. The thought of climbing the rope, or bouncing on the trampoline, or doing calisthenics naked as Danny Kaye sang *"Go, you chicken fat, go!"* from the record player, horrified me. What was this place called Harrad? Did people ever really feel comfortable enough to swim naked? In front of other people? Did people ever feel comfortable enough to be naked at all?

Yet the character Harry writes:

"Every day when I go to Physical Education, there they are . . . girls . . . naked, swimming in the pool, playing volleyball . . . yelling, screaming, soprano-joyous." One day, his classmate Sheila plops down beside him at the edge of the pool, water dripping from her breasts, and tells him: *"You know just two weeks ago when I first came here and had to walk out in front of everyone naked, I thought I'd die of embarrassment. Now it seems the only way to be . . . naked."* Really? I thought when I read that. Someday *I* might feel comfortable walking around naked? The idea seemed both impossible and exciting. And very, very far away.

■ ■ ■ ■

A couple of years before I read *The Harrad Experiment,* a boy approached me on the stretch of asphalt that served as our playground, and said, "You want to go out with me?" "Going out" meant that you wore his ID bracelet, stood by the fence with him every morning before school and again after lunch, and maybe met him at the mall on Saturdays. My parents would absolutely kill me if I went out with a boy, even in this benign fashion. Yet the idea that a boy liked me made me consider the offer. This boy was tall and broad-shouldered, dark-haired and strong-jawed. He was also several years older than anyone else in our grade, having stayed back a rumored three times. He wore a leather jacket, short black Beatles boots, tight jeans, and a scowl that was almost frightening. And *he* liked *me*? The girl who raised her hand too much in class, wore glasses, and carried around books the size of bricks?

Before I could answer "Okay!" he said, "If you go out with me, you gotta stop using so many big words. No one likes a girl who uses so many big words."

My vocabulary, honed by taking the monthly *Reader's Digest* "How to Improve Your Word Power" test and reading books far beyond my ken, was one of the things of which

I was most proud. To not use it seemed almost a punishment. I guess I took too long to think about his offer because he looked at me in disgust and said, "Ah, forget it. You just like big words, not me."

When I read Ruth's observation to Stanley in *The Harrad Experiment,* "*Anyway, darned few men want to marry a brainy woman. They want somebody to tell them they are wonderful, and be ready to cuddle with them or baby them,*" I thought of that boy. Was it true that all boys were like him? Stanley does suggest to Ruth that perhaps a girl could be cuddly and intelligent, but Ruth responds, "*Sure, intelligent. She can read the bestsellers and take on little civic problems in her women's* club . . . but let her really get her own interests . . . let her not be completely children and house oriented . . . then watch out, she's in for trouble." Later in the novel, Beth describes love like this: "Love is something else . . . Something more dynamic, all consuming. Something that makes you want to kneel down before somebody, humble yourself to him. Give yourself irrevocably." These debates, which continue throughout the novel, articulated my own confusion about sex and love. What was the difference? How did I know if the feelings I had were sexual ones or real love? Was it really okay to have many sexual partners and someday think, as Valerie does, "Sometimes I wake up *in the night and for a sleepy moment I may forget whether I am with Stanley, Jack or Harry, and then I feel warm and bubbly."*

Yes, *The Harrad Experiment* helped me, a sexually naïve, even prudish fourteen-year-old girl, to put words to all I was wondering about in the shifting values of the 1970s. But arguably more important, it told me how sex worked, what actually went on between a man and a woman when they made love, what went where and how it felt. The pages that I read over and over — pages 160 to 167 — were exactly what I needed to understand. Reading them made me blush and squirm uncomfortably, but they also empowered me. Finally I understood.

The scene involves two characters who are practicing a method of sexual intercourse called sexual communion, a concept based on Hindu Tantric literature. Before Sheila and Stanley try sexual communion, Rimmer introduces philosophical and historical information about it. The basic idea is for a couple to delay orgasm — a word whose meaning I had to run to the dictionary to find. "A climax of sexual excitement, characterized by feelings of pleasure centered in the genitals and (in men) experienced as an accompaniment to ejaculation." *What?* I thought when I read that. *Pleasure in the genitals?* I remember slamming the fat dictionary shut, sitting on my bed, and trying to absorb what I'd just read.

But this scene between Sheila and Stanley made it all seem less scary, less confusing, and even exciting. Stanley enters her and they lie side by side reading to each other. At one point, Sheila tells him she's about to explode, at which point I realized that women get to enjoy this too. For seven pages, they read out loud and touch each other and shift positions, until finally, on page 167, they can't take it anymore. The book falls to the floor with a thud, and Stanley tells Sheila he's past the point of no return. To my surprise and delight, it's Sheila who kisses him wildly and shouts, *"Oh, God! Darling . . . darling . . . so have*

I. So have I!"

Like so many of the 1950s values
and ideas on which I'd been raised,
sex had been challenged in this
changing world I was living in, *The
Harrad Experiment* brought me
headfirst into understanding — and
almost ready to join — the sexual
revolution of the 1970s. A fear of
pregnancy, the wrath of my mother,
disappointing Jesus, and a general
"good girl" hang-up kept me safely
innocent and relatively pure
through high school. It was years
before I felt comfortable being
naked, years before I had my first
sexual relationship, years before I
fell in love. Yet it was a book that
taught me about sex and love and
how to not confuse the two, a book

that told me what even my sex ed
teacher and my mother could not.

LESSON 9: HOW TO SEE THE WORLD

DOCTOR ZHIVAGO

BY BORIS PASTERNAK

I grew up listening to my father's stories of his days in the navy. He described Lombard Street in San Francisco — *the crookedest street in the world!* — and how in the tropics it would rain on only one side of the street. He told me again and again his stories about how in Morocco he once ate dog for dinner — *they starved the dog for a week, then fed it rice, and then killed it and cooked it, and the rice was the stuffing, right inside the dog!* — and in China he ate "hundred-year" eggs, which were buried and preserved and smelled and tasted rancid — *they made me gag but I had to eat them. You can't insult your hosts.* He skied in Greece; he stood at the railing of a ship and threw pennies into the Caribbean off the coast of Haiti for children to dive for and collect; when he lived in Naples he drove a Fiat Topolino, which was the smallest car in the world; in China he saw people die in the street from starvation. And I, the little girl on his big lap, tracing the tattoo of an eagle in front of a setting sun on his forearm, wanted to do all of those things and more. California and Morocco and

Greece and Italy and China . . .
"Where else?" I used to ask him.
He smelled of Old Spice and Vi-
talis and Ivory soap and cigarettes.
"In Cuba I was bit by a mongoose,"
he told me, "and I had to go into
the hospital and get rabies shots
right in my stomach."

Where else? There was always,
always somewhere else.

But mostly we stayed put.

My mother did not like to travel.
She did not like to leave her own
mother, who had a vague heart ail-
ment and always seemed close to
death, though she lived until she
was eighty or eighty-two or eighty-
three (no one really knew, because
they'd changed her birth date so
she could go to work in the mills

sooner). Every other summer we four — Mom, Dad, my brother Skip, and me — got into our green Chevy station wagon and drove to Indiana to visit my father's family. To make it exciting each time we stopped at a different attraction — Niagara Falls; Hershey, Pennsylvania; Amish country; Montreal. I thought it was exciting anyway, leaving Rhode Island and driving through six other states, sleeping in motels with pools that reeked of chlorine and beds that shook if you put a dime in them. My mother packed a cooler with fried chicken and sodas and kept Underwood deviled ham and potato chips in a bag at her feet. But the night we stopped at the motel we ate out, maybe at a Howard Johnson's or Cracker Barrel, and we got to order anything we wanted. Once, in Montreal, we ate at a steakhouse and Skip, who had just started to learn French in school, ordered *petits pois* and *bifteck,* impressing us all; in Niagara Falls we ate in a restaurant at the top of a building that slowly rotated, a feat of engineering that dazzled me.

I carefully wrote down all the license plates I saw, wishing I lived in New Mexico for its yellow-and-red one with LAND OF ENCHANTMENT on it, or Colorado with its green license plate and white snow-capped mountains at the bottom. After one trip, I wrote to the governor of Rhode Island and suggested we change from our dull black-and-white plate to a blue one with whitecapped waves. He never wrote back. But that was how great my desire for somewhere special was, I would design a new license plate just to make my little state stand out somehow.

My hometown of West Warwick had once been special, long before I was born. In 1809, the Lippitt Mill was built there, and it holds the distinction of being the second-oldest mill in the state, and one of the oldest textile mills in America. And Fruit of the Loom was born in my town in 1865, eventually having more than one thousand looms at work in its mill. But when I was a kid, the biggest mill had long since burned down, and many of the other mills that lined the polluted Pawtucket River had closed. We had a main street, with a square stone town hall and a square stone post office and a square stone bank that stayed open late on Friday evenings. There were two women's shops and one men's — Maxine's, Seena's, and St. Onge; a Newberry's five-and-dime with a lunch counter, cages of parakeets, and bins of notions; Irene's, a hat shop, where my mother got the hats she wore to church (this was her standard Mother's Day gift until Irene's closed); and the Palace Theatre, where for thirty-five cents my cousins and I saw double-feature matinees like *A Hard Day's Night* and

Up the Down Staircase. There was a New York System too, a Rhode Island oddity that sells special small hot dogs — *hot wieners* — in steamed buns with a secret meat sauce, chopped onions, mustard, and celery salt on top. Usually a person would eat three hot wieners, except my brother and father who ate six or even nine.

But by the time I was in ninth grade, although the square stone buildings and the New York System remained, everything else was gone, the buildings boarded up, the XXX movie theater replacing my beloved Palace Theatre. St. Onge had moved to the new mall, the other stores had simply vanished. Even though my father still went to the bank on Friday evenings, he came right home. No more window-shopping or ducking into Newberry's for shiny buttons or artificial flowers for my mother to arrange as a centerpiece. Living in what I saw as a dead-end town, I wanted, even more than ever, to *go.* I wanted to eat dog stuffed with rice in Morocco and go skiing in Greece.

Then I found the perfect novel sitting on the library shelf: *Doctor Zhivago* by Boris Pasternak. At 1,059 pages, it didn't so much sit on the shelf as dominate it. And the title — the mysterious combination of *Zh* . . . I tried to imagine how to pronounce it. Like *Shh?* Like *Za?* The writer's name too: *Boris.* I lived in a world of Michaels and Stevens and Johns; Vinnys and Tonys and Joes. The only Boris I'd ever heard of was Boris Badenov from *Rocky and Bullwinkle.* So I knew that this writer was Russian. Somehow even then, as a thirteen-year-old girl who knew almost nothing, I did know the magic of books. I understood as I held that hefty book in my hands, staring at the unusual cover — a drawing of a small house in a snowy field with a horse-drawn carriage approaching, all of it covered with what looked like a child's crayoned lines in mustard, mauve, and teal — that this Russian novel would transport me from my own little town to Russia, a place about which I knew nothing except that they had nuclear bombs pointed at us, they were Communists, and just the summer before they had invaded Czechoslovakia — Mama Rose and I had watched on television as the tanks rolled down the streets of Prague.

There had been a movie of *Doctor Zhivago* five years earlier, with Omar Sharif and Julie Christie. My parents had walked out halfway through — too slow, too boring, too long, too much snow. But the novel — the novel! — was none of these things. At least, not to me. It was confusing, jumping in time and point of view. Vladimir Nabokov called *Doctor Zhivago* "a sorry thing, clumsy, trite and melodramatic, with stock situations, voluptuous lawyers, unbelievable girls, romantic robbers, and trite coincidences." Reviewers described it as "having no real plot, confused chronology, oddly effaced main characters, and contrived coincidences." All of which is true, even though Boris Pasternak won the 1958 Nobel Prize for Literature shortly after *Doctor Zhivago* was published.

I admit that I loved those coincidences that Nabokov and many critics hated. I loved how Yuri could end up in the same town as Lara and wander into the library and see her there, or how Yuri gets wounded and is a patient, and later a doctor, in the military hospital where Lara is a nurse. I believed, or wanted to believe, in chance encounters, true love, and romance. I was confused by the characters, all of whom had three names and even nicknames, almost impossible to keep straight. But that didn't really matter to me because all I cared about was Lara and Yuri, their unrequited love. How he looked at her in wonder and amazement! How he vowed to try not to love her! But love is stronger than that, Pasternak told me. Yuri couldn't resist. And ever so briefly, Lara is his.

In his introduction to a reissue of the novel, John Bayley wrote: "The best way to understand *Doctor Zhivago* is to see it in terms of this great Russian literary tradition, as a fairy tale." Except in *this* fairy tale, no one lives happily ever after. Yuri Zhivago dies alone in Moscow; Lara dies in a gulag during Joseph Stalin's Great Purge; their daughter, Tanya, abandoned in the Urals by her mother when she was a child, is a laundress.

Perhaps ultimately *Doctor Zhivago* was what it never intended to be, as Richard Pevear wrote in his introduction: "a moving love story set against the grim realities of twentieth-century Russian history." The novel opens in 1903 at the funeral of Yuri's mother and moves from there to the Russian Revolution of 1905, the civil war, World War I, and World War II, with uprisings and protests and skirmishes and Cossacks and the White Army and Tsarists and more throughout. So many historical events and facts that I had never heard of that I made a list while reading: *Nikitsky Gate, The Presma, Bourgeoisie, Faust, Komuch, Tolstoyan, Pushkin* . . . And I spent long afternoons looking up all of these things and more.

In school, we had studied American history and, that year, ancient Rome. But to me, Russia was a mysterious place with nuclear missiles pointed at us, a country I knew virtually nothing about. Until *Doctor Zhivago.* I read Pasternak's descriptions of the six-mile-long Kologrivov estate with sheaves of wheat and a river gleaming beyond "fields following fields" until they were lost in the distance. *"These vast expanses gave him [Yuri] a feeling of freedom and elation. They made him think and dream of the future."* Wasn't I too seeking that feeling of freedom? My town offered only the opposite; the mills and polluted river seemed to conspire to prevent elation.

We had no grand houses really; the town had streets lined with old mill houses and the triple-deckers the immigrants eventually bought. Even the newer developments, though neat and tree-lined, offered only small split ranches or colonials. To read about the Gromekos' house, with its top floor of bed-

rooms and studies and a boudoir
— *Boudoir!* Another word I had to
look up! — was intoxicating. My
own house was typical of the 1960s
makeovers: Formica and paneling,
artificial flowers and fruit, avocado
and harvest-gold accents. The
Gromekos' curtains were pistachio
colored, their upholstery olive
green, and their potted plants resembled seaweed *"like a green,
sleepily swaying seabed."*

The Gromekos hosted chamber
music with piano trios, string quar-
tets, and violin sonatas. So unlike
the Johnny Cash music my parents
played on our stereo, or the folk
records I played alone in my room!
Even the food Pasternak described,
the supper table *"white and long as*

a winter road," "the frosted bottles of red rowanberry cordial" and *"crystal cruets in silver stands"* transported me to a different world, a place completely unlike my home, with the tablecloth covered with plastic and the red sauce and meatballs and sausage — delicious and comforting and plentiful, certainly, but served on mismatched platters and bowls. No *"picturesque arrangements of game and zakuski* [yet another word to look up]" or *"baskets of mauve cineraria* [and another!] *smelling of almonds."* All of it — the golden domes of churches and the girls in white dresses on Whitsun Eve, the green birch saplings hung over the church railings, the potatoes covered with old blankets and hay in the cellar, even the Proclamations posted on doors describing the various rules and punishments under the Red Army — whetted my already big appetite for travel and adventure, for some other place, pointed my compass outward.

But *Doctor Zhivago* pointed me inward too, toward other Russian novels, like *Anna Karenina* and *War and Peace* by Leo Tolstoy; nonfiction books about Russia, like *The Gulag Archipelago* by Aleksandr Solzhenitsyn and *Nicholas and Alexandra* by Robert K. Massie; and toward epic novels in general. After I had devoured all of the Russians, I discovered Victor Hugo's *Les Misérables* and began the same obsession with French literature.

Like *Doctor Zhivago, Les Misérables* has its critics. At 1,232 pages (arguably the longest novel in European literature), it is described by *The Guardian* as a novel of "gargantuan length and exaggerated coincidences," in which "everything seems utterly improbable and every plot twist operates through coincidences: a father doesn't recognize his son, a criminal doesn't recognize a man he has pursued for years . . ." Even Hugo himself called *Les Misérables* "formidable, gigantic, colossal, monstrous." But these were the very things I loved about epic novels, which by definition center upon a hero and great events narrated in an elevated style. I loved nothing more than to lose myself in these gargantuan novels with their pages and pages of characters and stories and settings and drama.

By the time I read *Les Misérables,* as a sophomore or junior in high school, I had also fallen in love with American literature of the 1920s (How? I cannot really say except once again I serendipitously discovered Fitzgerald and Hemingway on the library shelves), in particular with Zelda Fitzgerald (I read and reread the Nancy Milford biography that came out the following year) and her life in Paris. Hugo's novel was described by scholar Kathryn Grossman as "in many ways, a love affair with Paris."

While Hugo was in exile in Britain, Baron Haussmann razed the old Paris that Hugo loved, and that is the setting for *Les Misérables;* a Paris of narrow streets and alleys and hidden neighborhoods that had existed since medieval times but was replaced with the broad avenues and open plazas we associate with the city today — a plan meant to eliminate the congestion that fostered diseases and to prevent the building of the very revolutionary barricades that Hugo describes.

Of course, *Les Misérables* led to my reading *The Hunchback of Notre-Dame* and *The Count of Monte Cristo* and to fall in love, as I had with Moscow and the Urals, with Paris, where in the Luxembourg Gardens *"the air was warm, the garden was inundated with light and shade . . . the sparrows were giving vent to little twitters in the chestnut trees"* and where, at the Saint-Paul-Saint-Louis church in the Marais, *"people halted on the Rue Saint-Antoine to gaze through the windows at the orange flowers quivering on Cosette's head."* Hugo once said, "He who contemplates the depths of Paris is seized with vertigo. Nothing is more fantastic. Nothing is more sublime." His novel, written more than a century before a teenager in a small town in a small state read it, did just that for me.

During my high-school years, I

read my way across oceans and mountains, through history and politics and cultures, into epic tales of love and sorrow and bravery and passion. These stories opened doors that led me out and ultimately away from home, fueled by the hope of glimpsing golden domes and rose windows of cathedrals; labyrinth streets and fields of wheat; of glimpsing this big, beautiful world that I began to imagine on my father's knee, and then began to almost grasp with a book in my hands.

"He who sees Paris," Victor Hugo wrote in *Les Misérables, "seems to see all history through with the sky and constellations in the intervals."* How similar to what Yuri says in

Doctor Zhivago: "*The roof over the whole of Russia has been torn off, and we and all the people find ourselves under the open sky.*" The sky. Endless and full of possibilities, the door to the past and to the future. Somehow I understood this as I read. And all these years later, if my father were still here beside me, I could tell him, "Look, Daddy, I have seen Paris and Beijing and Istanbul. I have gazed at the Great Pyramid and the Himalayas and Machu Picchu. I have eaten yak and horse and deep-fried crickets. Thank you for showing me the world that books helped me imagine." If only he and Hugo and Pasternak and everyone who pointed me toward the sky could know I am still looking upward.

LESSON 10: HOW TO RUN AWAY

RABBIT, RUN

BY JOHN UPDIKE

Here I am, the girl who used to sit on the small landing at the top of the stairs that led to our bedrooms and stare out the window there. When I look back at that girl, I picture her there. I could see rooftops of houses, including my uncle Joe's across the street; when the trees were bare I could see all the way to the mall; on clear days I could see the community college buildings and vague roofs in the next town. I played a game: *Some-*

day, I will go beyond all of these buildings. Beyond Providence, which was ten miles away. Beyond Boston, which was fifty miles away. *Someday, I will go farther than I can even imagine.* Farther than anyone can imagine. I meant that both literally — I would leave this small town, this small state, New England, maybe even the United States — and figuratively. How far I wanted to go!

As I watched cousins getting married in heavy white beaded wedding gowns, I vowed to wear champagne or even pink. Their husbands were all nice guys from town who ran delis or worked at Electric Boat or as electricians or plumbers. I would find a poet, I decided, maybe even someone from England or France. We would name our children Summer or Sage, live by the beach or in a loft. We, *I*, would be different.

Much of this thinking I attribute to growing up in the 1960s. Around me, the world changed while I watched. Men still wore hats; teenagers grew their hair long. My mother wiggled herself into a girdle every morning; other women burned their bras. People bucked the system, lived on the land, had sex before marriage, hitchhiked, bought Eurail passes and backpacks while fathers still pulled their Chevys into their driveways at five o'clock and walked into a home they'd bought with a wife making dinner and two kids watching television. We Shake 'n Baked our pork chops, made Hamburger Helper, and ate TV dinners, but health food stores were opening and there were suddenly granola and yogurt and lentil burgers. All of it confused me. Where did I fit into this shifting landscape?

This question haunted me for many years. I considered marriage young, but opted to move away and live alone in a city. I considered going to graduate school, but instead went to work for TWA as a flight attendant. Always a push and pull, never certain I'd chosen the right way, which most times was the unconventional one. Recently I heard Gloria Steinem interviewed by Terry Gross on *Fresh Air,* and she described the cause of her mother's depression as patriarchal tyranny. I wished I could point to something like that for what I'd always felt, but nothing fit. That yearning I could not name, the same one that kept me looking out that window as a teenager, never left me.

To me, one movie and one novel captured what I felt, and I turned to them again and again for validation and even solace that I wasn't alone with this feeling. *The Graduate* came out in 1967, and while I'm certain I didn't see it when I was only ten years old (even though my parents never restricted what movies I saw or what books I read,

I doubt even they would have let me go see *The Graduate*), I know I did see it young, at thirteen or fourteen, perhaps at the Midland Cinema. Oddly, our mall had a small movie theater that showed foreign and independent films. I loved going there, loved how what I saw often confused or embarrassed me, how the movies there made me think in ways that only books did. I saw *Women in Love* and *Le Genou de Claire* and, I think, a rerelease of *The Graduate* in 1970 or '71. From the moment Dustin Hoffman's face appears in close-up as the airline captain announces landing and Simon and Garfunkel start singing "The Sound of Silence," I loved that movie. I thought, as crazy as it sounds, that it was a movie about me.

Around the same time I read a novel about a young man who wants to escape, who wants freedom from the moral and societal expectations placed on him, who wants to run. I had never even heard of John Updike when I took the green, yellow, and blue striped book off the library shelf. But just like that opening sequence of *The Graduate,* the opening pages of *Rabbit, Run* drew me in and held on to me until its final words: *"His hands lift of their own and he feels the wind on his ears even before, his heels hitting heavily on the pavement at first but with an effortless gathering out of a kind of sweet panic growing lighter and quicker and quieter, he runs. Ah: runs. Runs.*" From my perch at the top of the stairs, that's what I imagined. Running.

Rabbit, Run was published in 1960, over a decade before I read it. John Updike said that when he looked around in 1959, he saw a number of scared, dodgy men who could not make commitments, men who had peaked in high school and existed in a downward spiral. Their idea of happiness, Updike noted, was to be young. Harry Angstrom, *Rabbit, Run*'s eponymously nick-named protagonist, is only twenty-six, yet on page two of the novel he refers to himself as old. Updike himself was only twenty-eight when he wrote the book. At the age of fourteen, I was more than willing to accept that Rabbit was indeed old. Twenty-six? Definitely old. In fact, rereading the novel recently I was stunned by how young he actually is in it because he *feels* so old, so disheartened and beaten.

A former high-school basketball star, Rabbit is married with one young son and a baby on the way, working at a job selling a kitchen gadget called a MagiPeel when the story opens. Julian Barnes described Angstrom in an article about all four Rabbit books in *The Guardian:* "Harry is site-specific, slobbish, lust-driven, passive, patriotic, hard-hearted, prejudiced, puzzled, anxious. Yet likeable — for his humour, his doggedness, his candor, his curiosity and his wrongheaded judgments — for example preferring Perry Como to Frank Sinatra." The description is fitting; yet as a young reader I developed a literary crush on Rabbit, as I did on Dr. Zhivago and Jay Gatsby. The allure of Zhivago and Gatsby is obvious. Angstrom — hard-hearted and anxious man that he is — less so. But in his introduction to *Rabbit Angstrom: A Tetralogy,* Updike himself comes close to capturing what I found so appealing in Rabbit: "The character of Harry 'Rabbit' Angstrom was for me a way in — a ticket to the America all around me . . . an Everyman who, like all men, was unique and mortal."

In my blue-collar mill town, I recognized Rabbit's own hometown of Brewster, and the people who populated it. "My subject," Updike said, "is the American-Protestant small-town middle class. I like middles. It is in middles that extremes crash, where ambiguity restlessly rules." Rabbit and I wanted to escape the very small town, the very middles, that Updike described. That ambiguity fed our restlessness, and therein lies the effect Rabbit had on my teenage self. He is, after all, a middle-class guy who is *overwhelmed by the shifting world around him.*" So overwhelmed that Rabbit does exactly what I dreamed of at the top of the stairs — he runs away. *"He had thought, he had read, that from shore to shore all America was the same."* He wonders, *"Is it just these people I'm outside, or is it all America?"* As the *New York Times* put it in their November 6, 1960, book review of *Rabbit, Run* it's "a tender and discerning study of the desperate and the hungering in our midst." If ever a word was perfect to describe how Rabbit and I felt, that word is *hungering.*

Isn't this the magic of books? That a fourteen-year-old girl can exactly identify with the fictional character of a twenty-six-year-old, married, former basketball star from Pennsylvania just as readily as that same girl — Italian American, blue-collar, Catholic in a small town — exactly identifies with Marjorie Morningstar, an upper-middle-class Jewish girl in New York City? When I read *Rabbit, Run,* I understood that Rabbit, and John Updike, knew me. The me I didn't think anyone else saw.

John Updike left New York City in 1957 for Ipswich, Massachusetts, because, as he said, "I was full of a Pennsylvania thing I wanted to say," and he could not write that in the city. The novel, written entirely in present tense and with multiple points of view, has an urgency made even more apparent by all the ways in which Harry runs. After he joins young boys in a basketball game at the start of the book (a scene that Updike imagined cinematically, with the title and credits playing above it), Rabbit runs home: *"Running,"* the paragraph begins, and then we get a description of the street where he lives as he is *"running uphill,"* with its *"block of big homes, small fortresses of cement and brick,"* and then halfway up the block *"a development built all at once in the thirties,"* until finally, *"There are a dozen three-story homes, and each has two doors. The seventh is his."* It is there on the worn wooden steps that Rabbit finally pauses.

"Don't run off on me," his wife,

Janice, admonishes him. Janice, who *"just yesterday, it seems to him, she stopped being pretty."* Janice, who, in one of the most harrowing scenes I have ever read to this day, gets drunk and accidentally drowns their infant daughter Rebecca in the bathtub while Rabbit has, once again, run off on her. And he runs from her again at Rebecca's funeral: *"He hates his wife's face. She doesn't see . . . A suffocating sense of injustice blinds him. Again he turns and runs."* Not just runs, but *"uphill exultantly. He dodges among gravestones."* Perhaps escaping the death of his soul that he so acutely feels but can't articulate. *"I'll tell you,"* Rabbit says, *"when I ran from Janice I made an interesting discov-*

ery . . . *if you have the guts to be yourself, other people'll pay your price."*

After I read *Rabbit, Run,* I read the other three John Updike books on the library shelf: *The Centaur, Couples,* and *Bech: A Book.* Although I remember being equal parts shocked and seduced by *Couples,* none of these other books had the effect on me that *Rabbit, Run* did. I took that book out of the library over and over, growing more certain with each reading that Updike had stared unflinchingly straight into my heart.

In 1974, I graduated from West Warwick High School in a ceremony held in the Warwick Musical Theatre, a giant tent on Route 2 that hosted the likes of Engelbert Humperdinck, John Davidson, and Liberace on summer nights. That fall, my parents drove me and my brand-new stereo thirty-one miles south to the University of Rhode Island and my new home in the Barlow dormitory, Room 401. For one day, I was a journalism major. When the teacher told us that in journalism we had to tell the truth — "No making things up!" — I immediately switched my major to English. In 1974, at URI, there were no creative writing classes, only remedial writing classes. My first English class was a general American literature survey. The teacher handed out the syllabus, and to me the reading list was like a gift. Someone had chosen all of these books for me to read. I didn't have to scour library shelves and haphazardly select books anymore. Here was *My Ántonia* by Willa Cather, *The Falconer* by John Cheever, *Humboldt's Gift* by Saul Bellow, and — I blinked to be sure I was reading it correctly — *Rabbit Redux* by John Updike.

As if she'd read my mind, the teacher asked, "How many of you have read John Updike's *Rabbit, Run*?"

I alone raised my hand.

She smiled at me, and gave me a little nod.

"The rest of you read *Rabbit, Run* first, before *Rabbit Redux*," she said.

My heart was beating hard against my ribs. For my whole teenage life, I'd read to understand who I was and where I was going and what it was I was yearning for so desperately. And sitting in that warm, stuffy classroom in Independence Hall on that September day in 1974, I realized I'd somehow, through serendipity and curiosity and doggedness and intelligence and just plain luck, done it right. I'd taught myself how to live the life I'd dreamed by reading books.

Soon I had other English classes, and professors who told me to read Shakespeare, Anne Sexton, Flannery O'Connor, and so many more authors that I cannot even begin to name them all. I discovered *The*

New Yorker, and the *New York Times Book Review,* and I made friends who loved to read, and then friends who wanted to write, and then I was doing it, living this life I'd dreamed about. I stepped into this big, beautiful world with an open, eager heart. I opened my arms to it, all of it.

This is why we all read, isn't it? To know the world and ourselves better. To find our place in that world. Even if you did have access to readers and guidance on what to read, even if you grew up in a family that loved to read and owned shelves of books, still, still, one day a book falls into your hands — perhaps it's *Beloved* or *A Wrinkle in Time* or *A Tree Grows in Brooklyn;*

perhaps it's *Great Expectations* or *Pride and Prejudice* — whatever book it is, it falls into your hands at just the right moment when you need to read it. It transforms you. Perhaps it lifts you up when you are at your lowest; perhaps it shows you what love is, or what it feels like to lose love; perhaps it brings you places far away or shows you how to stay put when you need to.

In a 1966 *Paris Review* interview, John Updike said, "When I write, I aim in my mind not toward New York but toward a vague spot a little to the east of Kansas. I think of the books on library shelves, without their jackets, years old, and a countryish teenaged boy finding them, and having them speak to him."

I was more than a little east of Kansas, and a daughter of Italian immigrants, but those books on library shelves called out to me too. Thick, beautiful old books. They called out, and I heard them. Gratefully, I heard them.

ACKNOWLEDGMENTS

I would like nothing more than to thank every writer who helped me become the person I used to dream of becoming, but the list would be too long and never ending.

Many, many thanks to my brilliant agent, Gail Hochman, who recognized how books had shaped me and urged me to write about that; and to my brilliant editor, Jill Bialosky, who agreed.

As always thanks to all the people at Brandt and Hochman and

W. W. Norton who work tirelessly for me. And to Sam and Annabelle, my kids who are passionate readers too and put up with a mom who reads and writes all the time.

And to Michael, ybv.

ABOUT THE AUTHOR

Ann Hood is the editor of *Knitting Yarns: Writers on Knitting* and the best-selling author of *The Book That Matters Most, The Knitting Circle, The Red Thread, Comfort,* and *An Italian Wife,* among other works. She is the recipient of two Pushcart Prizes, a Best American Spiritual Writing Award, a Best American Food Writing Award, a Best American Travel Writing Award, and the Paul Bowles Prize

for Short Fiction. She lives in
Providence, Rhode Island.

The employees of Thorndike Press hope you have enjoyed this Large Print book. All our Thorndike, Wheeler, and Kennebec Large Print titles are designed for easy reading, and all our books are made to last. Other Thorndike Press Large Print books are available at your library, through selected bookstores, or directly from us.

For information about titles, please call:
(800) 223-1244

or visit our website at:
gale.com/thorndike

To share your comments, please write:
Publisher
Thorndike Press
10 Water St., Suite 310
Waterville, ME 04901